China Branding

Martin J. Liu · Jun Luo
Editors

China Branding

Cases from Zhejiang

palgrave
macmillan

Editors
Martin J. Liu
University of Nottingham Ningbo China
Ningbo, Zhejiang, China

Jun Luo
University of Nottingham Ningbo China
Ningbo, Zhejiang, China

ISBN 978-981-13-9317-4 ISBN 978-981-13-9318-1 (eBook)
https://doi.org/10.1007/978-981-13-9318-1

This Palgrave Macmillan imprint is published by the registered company Springer Nature Singapore Pte Ltd.
The registered company address is: 152 Beach Road, #21-01/04 Gateway East, Singapore 189721, Singapore

Contents

Notes on Contributors

Dr. M. S. Balaji is an Associate Professor in Marketing and the Head of Department for EMM at Nottingham University Business School China. Balaji has published his research in leading marketing and business management journals including *Journal of Business Research*, *European Journal of Marketing*, *Information and Management*, *International Journal of Hospitality Management*, *Journal of Services Marketing*, *Service Industries Journal* and others.

Prof. Alain Yee Loong Chong is a Professor in Information Systems and Dean of Graduate School at University of Nottingham Ningbo China. He obtained his PhDs from University of Nottingham and Multimedia University Malaysia and was a postdoctoral research fellow at Hong Kong Polytechnic University. His current research interests include social media analytics, digital transformations and mobile computing. His work has appeared in *Journal of Association for Information Systems, European Journal of Operations Research, Information & Management, Decision Support Systems, Transportations Research Part B: Methodological, Annals of Operations Research, International Journal of Operations and Production Management, Information Systems Frontier*, among others. He now serves as the Co-Editor of *Industrial Management & Data Systems*, Senior Editor of *Decision Support Systems* and Associate Editor of *Information & Management.*

Dr. Xuan Feng is an Assistant Professor in Human Resource Management and Organizational Behaviour at Nottingham University Business School

China. Her academic and work expertise lands in the areas of assessment and development of ethically oriented leadership, employee experience and wellbeing, global employability and career development, international HRM, and global talent policy research.

Prof. Peter S. Hofman is Professor of Corporate Social Responsibility and Corporate Governance and Associate Dean for Academic Development at Nottingham University Business School China. He has published numerous articles, books, book chapters and reports on corporate social responsibility in Europe and China, innovation in Chinese SMEs, technology transfer and sustainable business strategies in academic outlets.

Yueqiu Hu is an assistant research fellow at Nottingham University Business School China. Before joining Nottingham University, she was a graduate student in Chinese University of Hong Kong. She finished her bachelor degree in Syracuse University with international relations and economics major in the United States. Her research interests include e-commerce, new retail, etc.

Dr. Lin Huang is a teaching fellow in Entrepreneurship at Nottingham University Business School China. Her research focuses on challenges entrepreneurs encounter in starting a business, and the determinants of company growth. Besides, she is also interested in supply chain management, especially in supply chain collaboration. Her project explored the configuration patterns of dyadic and triadic collaborations in supply chain network, and compared them through examples in different industries.

Yue Huang is an assistant research fellow at Nottingham University Business School. Prior to joining Nottingham University Ningbo China, she obtained her master degree of Imperative Business Economics from the University College London in 2017.

Prof. Martin J. Liu is a Professor in Marketing and Innovation and the Associate Dean for Research and Knowledge Exchange at Nottingham University Business School China. In addition, Martin has led the development for the "Zhejiang Provincial Branding Academy", a research and education platform cofounded by UNNC and Zhejiang Provincial Government in China. He is also a visiting professor at Warwick

University and serves as an external expert for many government agencies in China. His main research interests include digital innovation, consumer behavior, e-marketing and brand strategy. His research has been published in *MIS Quarterly, Journal of Business Research, International Journal of Production Research, Business History, Transportation Research Part E: Logistics and Transportation Review, International Journal of Production Economics* and others.

Paul C. Y. Liu has 15 years of experience in real estate development. He has developed, operated and sold 200,000 m^2 in commercial projects of shopping centers, offices towers and hotels JVs and 250,000 m^2 residential projects of luxury apartments, townhouses, villas in various cities of India, Vietnam, Singapore and China before joining UNNC in 2017.

Dr. Jun Luo is an Assistant Professor in Marketing & Entrepreneurship and the Deputy Director of Undergraduate Programmes at Nottingham University Business School China. Her research is in the area of services marketing. Her co-authored research output has appeared in both marketing and management journals, including *Journal of Business Research, International Journal of Production Economics*, and *Transportation Research Part E: Logistics and Transportation Review* etc.

Dr. Luis D. Torres is an Assistant Professor in Organisational Behaviour at Nottingham University Business School China, an Associate Director for SustainaValue in Chile, and a Fellow of the Institute of Corporate Responsibility and Sustainability in the UK. He has teaching and consulting experience in China, UK, Chile, and Spain. He is currently developing research and consultancy on business responsibility and sustainability in emerging markets.

Dr. Jie Wang is an Associate Professor in Organisational Behavior and the Director of Ph.D. Programme at Nottingham University Business School China. She has published academic articles in journals such as *Human Relations, Journal of Organizational Behavior, Human Resource Management*, and *Journal of Business Ethics.*

Dr. Liang (Lucas) Wang is an Assistant Professor in International Business and Strategy at Nottingham University Business School China. His research interests include strategic alliances, inter-firm cooperation across national borders and business sustainability.

Zi Wang obtained her master's degree in global marketing from the University of York in 2017 and now working as a Ph.D. candidate in marketing in the University of Nottingham Ningbo China. Her research interest includes consumer psychology, luxury consumption, sustainable marketing and business ethics.

Chenchen Weng is a research assistant at Nottingham University Business School China. She graduated from Durham University with the major of Strategic Marketing. Her research interests include digital innovation, customer service and value creation.

Dandan Ye is currently a doctoral researcher in Marketing and innovation at Nottingham University Business School China. Prior to this, she worked as a research assistant at the Nottingham University Business School. Her main research interests are in the areas of digital innovation, business transformation and social media communication.

Shengjing Yu is currently a doctoral researcher in IDIC at Nottingham University Business School China. Prior to this, she worked as a research assistant at the Nottingham University Business School. Her main research interests are in the areas of digital innovation and innovation strategy.

Dr. Cherry Yi Zhang is an Assistant Professor in Finance at Nottingham University Business School China. Her research interests are in the areas of capital market, empirical asset pricing, investment, anomalies, and corporate finance. She has published in the *Review of Finance* and *Journal of Economic Behavior and Organization.*

Dr. Tiantian Zhang is an Assistant Professor in Economics and Quantitative Methods, the Director of External Engagement, and senior research fellow at the Center for Inclusive Finance at Nottingham University Business School China. In the past, she worked at Cardiff Business School (2007–2011) as a teaching assistant and a research fellow in Julian Hodge Institute of Applied Macroeconomics, then at Shanghai Shipping Exchange (SSE) as a senior research fellow (2011–2012).

Shuning Zheng is a Ph.D. student of management information system at Nottingham University Business School China. Prior to joining UNNC, Shining did a M.Sc. at the University of Durham in Finance and Investment. Shuning's primary research interests include blockchain technology applications and fin-tech.

Dr. Abby Jingzi Zhou is an Assistant Professor in International Business and Strategy at Nottingham University Business School China. Her research broadly covers knowledge management and human resource management in the areas of international business. She has published numerous articles in knowledge management and international human resource management in both leading academic and practitioner journals.

Dr. Steven Shijin Zhou is an Assistant Professor in International Business and Strategy at Nottingham University Business School China. He has published numerous articles in innovation and knowledge management in both leading academic and practitioner journals and such as *Management and Organization Review*, *Asia Pacific Journal of Management*, *Journal of Management & Organization*, *Tsinghua Management Review*, and *Business Review*.

Dr. Fei Zhu is an Assistant Professor in Entrepreneurship at Nottingham University Business School China. She focuses on individual-level entrepreneurship research, in particular, entrepreneurial decision-making and its antecedents. Dr. Zhu uses experiment and survey in her research and has published papers in ABS 3&4 journals.

List of Figures

List of Tables

CHAPTER 1

Place Umbrella Branding and the Provision of Quality: A Case Study of the "ZhejiangMade" Brand

Shengjing Yu, Martin J. Liu and Dandan Ye

Introduction

Zhejiang province is a manufacturing center in China and the development of its manufacturing industry keeps on growing. It should be noted that a number of firms have already been equipped with the world-leading technical and quality management capabilities in producing their products; however, the majority of manufacturing firms in Zhejiang are in the low-end industrial chain with weak innovation capabilities and products with low added value which results in a low-profit margin, threatening their competitiveness, or even survival in the market. The Zhejiang provincial

S. Yu (✉) · M. J. Liu · D. Ye
University of Nottingham Ningbo China, Ningbo, China
e-mail: shengjing.yu@nottingham.edu.cn

M. J. Liu
e-mail: martin.liu@nottingham.edu.cn

D. Ye
e-mail: dandan.ye@nottingham.edu.cn

M. J. Liu and J. Luo (eds.), *China Branding*,
https://doi.org/10.1007/978-981-13-9318-1_1

government has started to become aware of the eliminating benefits of producing low-cost products. In order to win the battle for customers in both the domestic and international markets, the government intends to help firms to establish a new competitive advantage. In recent years, Chinese President Xi Jinping posited the strategy of "Three Transformations", which means transforming from Made in China to Created in China, from Chinese speed to Chinese quality, and from Chinese products to Chinese brands (CCTV.com 2017). Premier Li Keqiang has also advocated the "Made in China 2025" strategy (Chinanews.com 2015). The Zhejiang provincial government has employed a place branding strategy for improving the quality of products produced by Zhejiang manufacturing firms and promoting these firms and their products in the domestic and international markets.

The Zhejiang Provincial Party Committee and the People's Government of Zhejiang Province launched a strategy of "ZhejiangMade" brands and initiated the "ZhejiangMade" brand building system. Around two decades ago, the government started to become aware that place branding could be a useful instrument to accelerate the upgrading and transformation of the manufacturing industry. In 2004, Xi Jinping, who was the secretary of the Zhejiang Provincial Party Committee, proposed to develop a provincial brand and went on encouraging to develop a provincial brand by attaching great importance to improve the quality of products made in Zhejiang province (Quality and Technical Supervision Bureau of Zhejiang Province 2017). The Zhejiang provincial government then provided policy support to enhance the quality of products manufactured in Zhejiang. In recent years, the Zhejiang provincial government continues to accelerate the efforts to build a provincial brand and issued a series of policies which affirmed the important role of the "ZhejiangMade" brand and stated that this brand is established as a "golden brand" of the Zhejiang economy.

This chapter offers an overview of the "ZhejiangMade" brand and its building system and examines the literature on place umbrella branding. It goes on to look at what actions the government has taken to ensure the transfer of the parent brand to its brand partners and examine the development of the "ZhejiangMade" brand to get a better understanding of how umbrella branding could be a good strategy to convince consumers and firms of product quality.

Literature Review

A place brand, according to Keller (2008), is developed to create an image of a place and improve the positive value of the place through differentiating the products and services from that place. As Hanna and Rowley (2008) suggest, a place can be a location, a region, a city, or a country. Scholars sometimes approach place branding from the perspective of the country of origin. The investigation of how a country of origin impacts on product evaluation was started by Dichter (1962), when the globalization of manufacturing was intensified. Verlegh and Steenkamp (1999) regard country of origin as a cognitive cue; that is the consumer perceives the products based on the perception of the country where the product originated from. Some country of origin cues can be found explicitly in the products, such as "Made in China" labels, and the other country of origin cues are implied in the products, such as language (Leclerc et al. 1994; Usunier 2011). The country of origin is used as a product evaluation cue by consumers when they are not familiar with a country's product or other information of products is not easy to assimilate. Elaydi and Mclaughlin (2012) suggest that the firms should incorporate the origin of place to their capability development strategy and deliver products with the community's core values, customs, and norms to obtain competitive advantage. Charters and Spielmann (2014) list four types of place brand, including country brands, regional brands, destination brands, and territorial brands, and they also conclude that a strong territorial brand will be supported by an effective brand manager, the willingness to co-operate, a common mythology, and local engagement.

Place branding has similarities with product branding and corporate branding, regarding branding management and development (Anholt 1998, 2002; Balmer and Greyser 1998). Domeisen (2003) states that similar to a company brand, a place brand is developed based on the customer's perception of the quality. Frost (2004) suggests that the strategy for a place branding could follow the development path of company branding, such as creating a clearly defined vision, which needs to be shared with stakeholders. Establishing the link between brand image and brand identity is one of the main goals that place branding, product branding, or corporate branding intend to achieve. A brand identity means "a unique set of brand associations that the brand strategies aspire to create or maintain" (Aaker 1996, p. 68). Brand image is formed when the customers have their own understanding and brief of a brand based on the brand's product and non-product attributes (Iversen and Hem 2008). Place of origin of the brand is an essential piece of information that may create or alter the brand image in customers' perception (Thakor and Katsanis 1997). It should be mentioned that place branding, compared to product branding, is not only under the control of an authority and in fact a variety of stakeholders with conflicting interests are involved (Frost 2004).

Another essential strategy for firms to market their products is umbrella branding, by which a bundle of products is unified as a bond of quality using a firm's reputation (Wernerfelt 1988). In the same vein, umbrella branding serves to support the marketing of products and services as a bond in the reputation of a place (De Chernatony 2008). The goal of umbrella branding is firstly the reduction of risk when introducing new products, and secondly the quality perception improvement of new brand partners (Aaker 2006; Laforet and Saunders 1994; Roehm and Tybout 2006). According to researches in the marketing field, the customers' perception of the product quality of a brand's extension depends on their experiences of the parent products. Customers are able to adopt their experiences with the parent as a signal of the extended products when they are not perfectly informed about them. De Chernatony (2008) points out that the provenance association of the place image is the core of umbrella branding and the transfer of quality perception depends on the degree of the congruity of the parent and the extent of the brand. According to Häubl and Elrod (1999), the signaling theory indicates that the parent brand perception is influenced by the extension and the quality perceptions of products which share the same parent brand and how they affect each other. Hakenes and Peitz (2008) have a different opinion, that umbrella branding is a useful approach to demonstrate to customers the product quality, only when there are serious defections in the quality of the product. In addition, Spielmann and Williams (2016) state that a territorial brand is a type of regional umbrella brand and find that the individual brand makes an effort to interact with the overarching territorial brand and attaches itself to a place of origin in order to leverage the marketing resources of territorial brands.

"ZhejiangMade" Brand

The "ZhejiangMade" brand is a place brand for products and firms, representing the highest level of manufacturing industry in Zhejiang province. The "ZhejiangMade" brand building system adheres to the combination of market-oriented operation and government-led promotion. The main goal of the "ZhejiangMade" brand is to develop and promote the place brand,

Picture 1.1 The logo of "ZhejiangMade" brand

which indicates superior quality of products and strong competitiveness of firms.

"Pin" is the logo of the "ZhejiangMade" brand, shown in Picture 1.1. The "Pin" logo is the image identity of the advanced manufacturing industry in Zhejiang. The logo is authorized to the firms and products to use once they get the certification of the "ZhejiangMade" brand. These firms can use the "Pin" logo in advertising materials, product introductions, and other promotional materials and can mark the "Pin" label on certified products and related packages.

With the vision of "place brands, advanced standards, market certification, and international awareness", the "ZhejiangMade" brand building system emphasizes the improvement of the supply capability of high-quality and high-end products in the Zhejiang manufacturing industry (Quality and Technical Supervision Bureau of Zhejiang Province 2016). Firms with the "ZhejiangMade" brand adopt advanced management methods and standards to stabilize the manufacturing capability and maintain these standards in the domestic first-rate or international advanced level. Products that meet high standards and quality requirements are certified with the "ZhejiangMade" brand. The "ZhejiangMade" brand aims to get recognized by the market and by society with the impression of high-quality, independent technology, good service, and high reputation.

The Zhejiang provincial government uses standards and certifications as main approaches to develop the "ZhejiangMade" brand, to maintain the cohesive value of the "ZhejiangMade" brand among brand partners, and to keep the brand image in line with the brand identity. The structure of the "ZhejiangMade" brand system is illustrated in Fig. 1.1. The "ZhejiangMade" brand building system aims to promote products, firms,

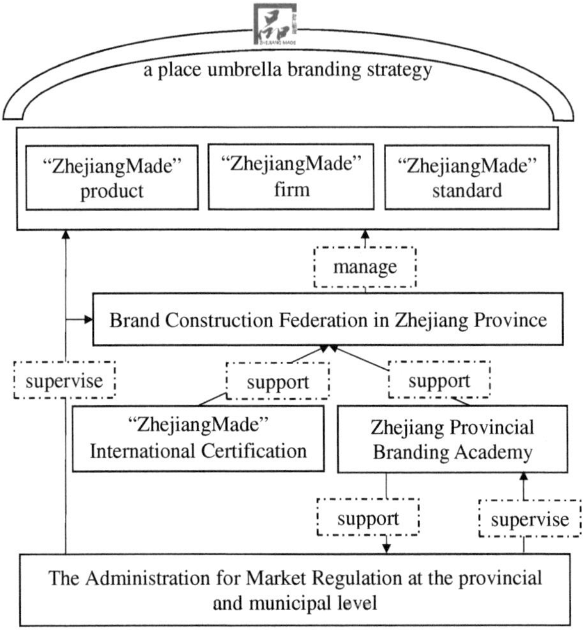

Source: Website of Brand Construction Federation in Zhejiang Province

Fig. 1.1 The framework of the "ZhejiangMade" brand system

and standards which satisfy the assessment requirments for the "Zhejiang-Made" brand. The Administration for Market Regulation at the provincial and municipal level leads and supervises the brand development. Brand Construction Federation in Zhejiang Province is the main party managing the brand development, with support from "ZhejiangMade" International Certification Alliance and Zhejiang Provincial Branding Academy. The "ZhejiangMade" brand was initiated in 2013. After several years' development, the "ZhejiangMade" brand developed significantly. Up until September 2018, 354 certificates of the "ZhejiangMade" brand were awarded to 195 firms, including 83 international mutual recognition certificates and 519 "ZhejiangMade" product standards (Zhejiang Provincial Administration for Market Regulation 2018).

Standard

The "ZhejiangMade" standard is developed with the aim to select firms with the ability to produce domestic leading or international advanced products. The "ZhejiangMade" standard system consists of "A + B" standards. Standard A is a general evaluation standard of the "ZhejiangMade" brand, which is illustrated in DB33/t 944-2014 "'ZhejiangMade' Evaluation Standard". Standard A is the foundation of the "ZhejiangMade" standard system. It defines the "ZhejiangMade" brand and requires the firm to satisfy the general and management terms to achieve "excellent quality, independent innovation, industrial collaboration, and social responsibility". Standard B is the main body of the "ZhejiangMade" standard system. It consists of product standards which are established by a group of parties. Brand Construction Federation in Zhejiang province collaborates with industrial leading firms, industry associations, relevant professional standardization committees, research institutes, inspection and testing institutions, certification agencies, universities, industry associations, and consumers to carry out activities such as establishing, evaluating, issuing, and implementing the standards. The product standard with the "ZhejiangMade" brand has requirements for the whole lifecycle of a product. A product with the "ZhejiangMade" standard has the characteristics of "careful design, excellent material selection, precise manufacture and meticulous service". All the product standards with the "ZhejiangMade" brand not only cover the basic mandatory production requirement but also have the requirement of key technical indicators. That demonstrates the technical level of "the best products from best enterprises" in China. The international standards are also adopted as reference to establish the standards of "ZhejiangMade" in order to prepare the standards system for making its way into the international market. The standard system of "ZhejiangMade" enhances the regional brand value and improves the overall competitiveness of the Zhejiang manufacturing industry.

There has been a rapid growth in the number of "ZhejiangMade" standards of products, shown in Fig. 1.2. Only 5 standards were established during the years 2012–2014. In 2015, there were 37 standards issued. The number of "ZhejiangMade" standards increased by more than 100 in 2016 and 2017. The number of product standards issued in 2018 was 628 and there were 921 "ZhejiangMade" product standards in total by the year of 2018.

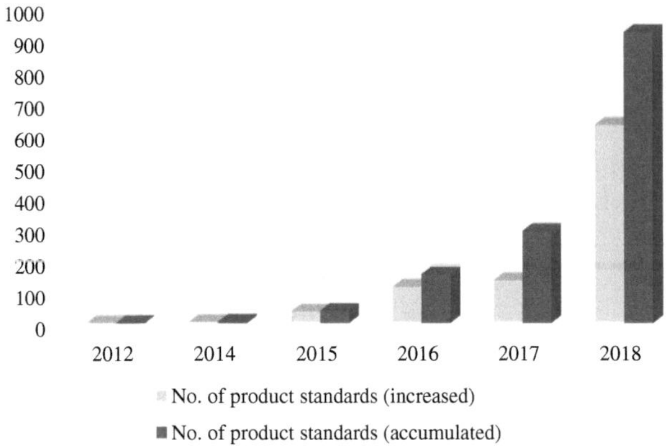

Source: Website of Brand Construction Federation in Zhejiang Province

Fig. 1.2 The growth of "ZhejiangMade" standards

The "ZhejiangMade" standard system covers a wide range of industries including the high-end equipment industry, energy-saving and environmental protection industry, transportation equipment industry, intelligent manufacturing industry, new materials and parts industry, consumer goods industry, traditional cultural and artistic works industry, pharmaceutical chemicals industry and so on. The "ZhejiangMade" standard system is spreading to more industries with the purpose of identifying firms which have the most advanced manufacturing capability so that other firms in the industry can improve products by meeting the "ZhejiangMade" standard.

Certification

Certification of product quality is a tool for a firm to convince consumers of their high quality (Hakenes and Peitz 2008). Another essential part of the "ZhejiangMade" brand building system is to issue the certification to firms and products. There are four main characteristics of products and firms with the "ZhejiangMade" brand. First, firms with the "ZhejiangMade" brand are required to employ performance excellence or other production management methods and the technical index of products should be taking the lead in the world. Second, firms with the "ZhejiangMade" brand must dominate their core technology and have the independent intellectual

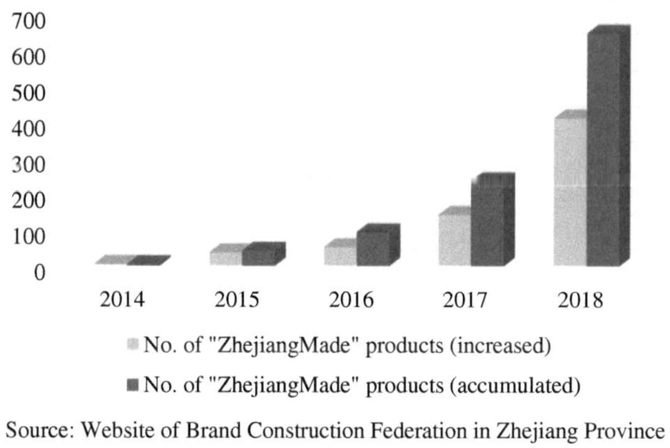

Fig. 1.3 The growth of the "ZhejiangMade" certificate

property rights of their products. Third, firms with the "ZhejiangMade" brand shall promote the coordination development of the industry chain in Zhejiang. Finally, these firms shall follow the principles of trustworthy and lawful operation and shall pay attention to their social responsibility including environmental improvement, resource protection, and public services.

Firms can apply for the "ZhejiangMade" certification for itself and its product. The certification is valid for three years. Once firms and products are certified by the "ZhejiangMade" brand, the firm is approved to use the "ZhejiangMade" "Pin" logo in advertising, product introductions, and other promotional materials. It should be mentioned that the international certification agencies are invited to help these firms to obtain international market recognition, strive to achieve "one certification, global recognition" and boost the competitiveness of the "ZhejiangMade" brand in the international market. The number of certification issued to products keeps on growing from the year of 2014, shown in Fig. 1.3. There were 648 "ZhejiangMade" certifications issued to products manufactured by firms in Zhejiang. Certification with the "ZhejiangMade" brand is an effective approach to ensure the products and firms to meet the vision of the "ZhejiangMade" brand and keep the brand value consistent among the brand partners.

Brand Manager

A capable brand manager is especially important for a successful place brand. According to Charters and Spielmann (2014), a business manager exerts their power over the place brand and ensures a common vision for the brand among stakeholders when the legitimacy of the business manager is acknowledged by the key players in the place. Zhejiang Provincial Administration for Market Regulation initiated the "ZhejiangMade" brand building system and established regulations and policies to develop the regional brand. With the support of government, Brand Construction Federation in Zhejiang province was established in 2016, and it is a non-profit third-party social organization responsible for developing and managing the "ZhejiangMade" brand. It consists of different organizations including leading firms in the Zhejiang manufacturing industry, universities and colleges, research institutes, as well as "ZhejiangMade" brand inspection and certification institutes. Brand Construction Federation in Zhejiang province is supported by the "ZhejiangMade" International Certification Alliance to provide a certification service to firms in Zhejiang. "ZhejiangMade" International Certification Alliance consists of nine domestic and international inspection and certification agencies. The alliance was set up in 2014 and issues product certifications and international mutual recognition certifications with the "ZhejiangMade" brand. Through improving the international mutual recognition of the "ZhejiangMade" brand, it aims to strengthen the validity of the "ZhejiangMade" brand, to improve the competitiveness of Zhejiang firms and products in the international market, and to accelerate industrial upgrading and economic transformation of the Zhejiang manufacturing industry. Brand Construction Federation in Zhejiang province also works with the Zhejiang Provincial Branding Academy, which provides education for individuals and firms for brand building through academic education and vocational skills training, and offers governments and firms a consultation and information service regarding brand building and promotion and so on.

A brand manager plays an essential role in the volume of supply, quality guarantee, reputation protection and general promotion of a brand (Charters and Spielmann 2014). In the delegation of the Zhejiang provincial government, the federation aims to improve the popularity and reputation of the "ZhejiangMade" brand through activities such as formulating and publishing standards, issuing brand certificates, formulating and publicizing standards, cultivating and protecting brand, publicity, promotion, and supervision. For example, Brand Construction Federation in Zhejiang province provides training courses of the "ZhejiangMade" brand to local firms and assists them in applying for a "ZhejiangMade" certification and in improving the manufacturing capability to produce products with excellent quality.

Concluding Remarks

The determining issue in place umbrella branding is how the brand is designed and developed and how the brand value is transferred to the stakeholders in the place. The Zhejiang provincial government began to implement a place umbrella branding strategy around a decade ago. Recently, with the intention of developing product quality as the new competitive advantage in the domestic and international markets, the government has developed the "ZhejiangMade" brand strategy in 2014 and carried out several actions, such as using standards and certificates as well as employing an effective brand manager to enhance the transference of brand value. In order to develop a sustainable and valuable brand, several concerns shall be mentioned. The government should keep on cooperating with the key players closely to ensure the consistency of policy support and improve the legitimacy of the brand manager. In addition, attention should be paid to the quality of products with the "ZhejiangMade" brand because the place brand value could be easily decreased by a lower quality product, which will reduce the credible reputation of the "ZhejiangMade" brand.

Further Investigation

1. What measures have been taken to promote the "ZhejiangMade" brand?
2. What is the relationship between the corporate brand and place umbrella brand?
3. What is the role of local government in place umbrella branding strategy?

References

Aaker, David A. *Building strong brands*. New York: The Free Press, 1996.

Aaker, David A. "Brand portfolio strategy." *Strategic Direction* 22, no. 10 (2006).

Anholt, Simon. "Nation-brands of the twenty-first century." *Journal of Brand Management* 5, no. 6 (1998): 395–406.

Anholt, Simon. "Foreward." *Journal of Brand Management* 9, no. 4/5 (2002): 229–239.

Balmer, John M. T., and Stephen A. Greyser. "Corporate marketing: Integrating corporate identity, corporate branding, corporate communications, corporate image and corporate reputation." *Journal of Marketing Management* 51, no. 3 (1998): 6–23.

CCTV.com. "Xi Jinping emphasized to learn and implement the spirit of the 19th National Congress of the Communist Party of China and promote the reform and development to keep up with the new era in his visit to Xuzhou, Jiangsu," 2017, accessed July 18, 2019. http://tv.cctv.com/2017/12/13/VIDEf8sb57AeR2lk7DU4FkSq171213.shtml.

Charters, Steve, and Nathalie Spielmann. "Characteristics of strong territorial brands: The case of champagne." *Journal of Business Research* 67, no. 7 (2014): 1461–1467.

Chinanews.com. "Li Keqiang: Implement the strategy of Made in China 2025 accelerate the shift to a manufacturing powerhouse," 2015, accessed July 18, 2019. http://www.chinanews.com/gn/2015/03-05/7103106.shtml.

De Chernatony, Leslie. "Adapting brand theory to the context of nation branding." In *Nation branding: Concepts, issues, practice*, 16–17. Oxford: Butterworth-Heinemann, 2008.

Dichter, Ernest. "The world customer." *The International Executive* 4, no. 4 (1962): 25–27.

Domeisen, Natalie. "Is there a case for national branding?" *International Trade Forum*, no. 1, p. 14. International Trade Centre, 2003.

Elaydi, Raed, and Josetta McLaughlin. "Cultivating terroir in subsistence markets: Development of terroir strategy through harmony-with-community framework." *Journal of Business Research* 65, no. 12 (2012): 1743–1748.

Frost, Randall. "Mapping a country's future." *Brandchannel. com* 19, 2004.

Hakenes, Hendrik, and Martin Peitz. "Umbrella branding and the provision of quality." *International Journal of Industrial Organization* 26, no. 2 (2008): 546–556.

Hanna, S., and J. Rowley. "An analysis of terminology use in place branding." *Place Branding & Public Diplomacy* 4, no. 1 (2008): 61–75.

Häubl, Gerald, and Terry Elrod. "The impact of congruity between brand name and country of production on consumers' product quality judgments." *International Journal of Research in Marketing* 16, no. 3 (1999): 199–215.

Iversen, Nina M., and Leif E. Hem. "Provenance associations as core values of place umbrella brands: A framework of characteristics." *European Journal of Marketing* 42, no. 5/6 (2008): 603–626.

Keller, Kevin Lane. *Strategic brand management: Building, measuring, and managing brand equity*. 2nd ed. Upper Saddle River: Prentice Hall. 2008.

Laforet, Sylvie, and John Saunders. "Managing brand portfolios: How the leaders do it." *Journal of Advertising Research* 34, no. 5 (1994): 64–77.

Leclerc, France, Bernd H. Schmitt, and Laurette Dubé. "Foreign branding and its effects on product perceptions and attitudes." *Journal of Marketing Research* 31, no. 2 (1994): 263–270.

Quality and Technical Supervision Bureau of Zhejiang Province. "To create the "ZhejiangMade" brand as the starting point, promote to build a province with strong standards, quality and brand," 2016, accessed July 18, 2019. http://mpnews.zjol.com.cn/system/2016/12/15/021399758.shtml.

Quality and Technical Supervision Bureau of Zhejiang Province. "The notice to implement the work of building and publicizing 'ZhejiangMade' brand conscientiously," 2017, accessed July 9, 2019. http://dangjian.people.com.cn/n1/2016/0810/c117092-28625516.html.

Roehm, Michelle L., and Alice M. Tybout. "When will a brand scandal spill over, and how should competitors respond?" *Journal of Marketing Research* 43, no. 3 (2006): 366–373.

Spielmann, Nathalie, and Christopher Williams. "It goes with the territory: Communal leverage as a marketing resource." *Journal of Business Research* 69, no. 12 (2016): 5636–5643.

Thakor, Mrugank V., and Lea Prevel Katsanis. "A model of brand and country effects on quality dimensions: Issues and implications." *Journal of International Consumer Marketing* 9, no. 3 (1997): 79–100.

Usunier, Jean-Claude. "Language as a resource to assess cross-cultural equivalence in quantitative management research." *Journal of World Business* 46, no. 3 (2011): 314–319.

Verlegh, Peeter W. J., and Jan-Benedict E. M. Steenkamp. "A review and meta-analysis of country-of-origin research." *Journal of Economic Psychology* 20, no. 5 (1999): 521–546.

Wernerfelt, Birger. "Umbrella branding as a signal of new product quality: An example of signalling by posting a bond." *The RAND Journal of Economics* 19, no. 3 (1988): 458–466.

Zhejiang Provincial Administration for Market Regulation. "The activity of 'ZhejiangMade' brand entering a new era is held in Hangzhou," 2018, accessed September 20, 2018. http://www.zjbts.gov.cn/HTML/zjdt/201809/f9680b88-8d6a-49ee-a6d8-cbcfca753d03.html.

CHAPTER 2

Branding in the Context of Globalization: A Case Study of Baoxiniao

Lin Huang, Jun Luo and Luis D. Torres

Introduction

In a more competitive business environment, branding is vital in assembling and maintaining a mix of values which are important to a company. Branding can be used as a powerful method to distinguish the goods and/or services of one manufacturer from those of another (Murphy 1988), where brands are treated as the lifeblood of companies (Steenkamp 2014). A number of established brands, which have come a long way in construction, are becoming increasingly strong through global expansion. It puts pressure on existing brands and latecomer brands (Hamin et al. 2014) to survive, especially on the ones from emerging markets. However, it is still challenging for them in acquiring values added to the established brand and pursuing sustained economic growth. Normally, a successful brand takes a long time to develop (Jim Wu 2009). Hunt (2019) argued that brands would influence companies' competitiveness, as a brand is a resource that has value to some market segments. Merz et al. (2018) defined this value

L. Huang (✉) · J. Luo · L. D. Torres
University of Nottingham Ningbo China, Ningbo, China
e-mail: Lin.Huang@nottingham.edu.cn

M. J. Liu and J. Luo (eds.), *China Branding*,
https://doi.org/10.1007/978-981-13-9318-1_2

as the perceived value attributable to the brand which would regulate customers' loyalty behavior positively at a superordinate level (Yeh et al. 2016); and in order to strengthen the brand, customer value is regarded as the cornerstone.

"Made in China" or "China made" is well-known all around the world, but many "China Brands" are little-known. Some scholars have argued that consumer knowledge and country of origin would affect consumers' evaluations of products (Schaefer 1997; Laforet and Chen 2012), where most consumers, when confronted, tend to choose a familiar local brand name. Besides, Steenkamp (2014) pointed out that due to linguistic differences between Asian and Western languages, the Chinese brand name could be difficult to pronounce and replicate, and/or be meaningless to their global consumers. Therefore, Chinese brands are recommended to develop their brand familiarity in target international markets and to build the brand knowledge of their potential customers, as it could influence consumers' purchase intentions (Laforet and Chen 2012). As the quality of products made in China has long been criticized, some consumers hold a negative image of China (Laforet and Chen 2012); therefore to build up the brand reputations with high-quality products is crucial to those Chinese brands that are striving to take the market from rivals globally.

This chapter attempts to evaluate the importance of branding in the development of a business and discuss how to do branding in the context of globalization with an example of Baoxiniao. The sections will begin with the branding relevant concepts and some case background information, and then move to the customer values appreciated by companies; finally, the strategic brand management in different business stages for further development will be stated.

Corporate Brand vs Product Brand

A corporate brand refers to the brand used for a company as a whole, which can sometimes also be known as the trade name (Li et al. 2016), and involves values that distinguish it from other competitors (Vallaster and Lindgreen 2011). Silva et al. (2017) argue that the corporate brand is a valuable strategic resource typically founded on the fundamental core values central to the company's character (Voss and Mohan 2016), which has the potential to create competitive advantages. Tarnovskaya et al. (2008) state that corporate branding needs to consider the interests of various stakeholders, where corporate brand is the balancing force that should be able to meet stakeholders' expectations and make them feel involved in establishing the brand (Hoque 2016). There is a relatively comprehensive definition of corporate branding given by Enwiller and Will (2002), which states that it is an "implemented process of creating and maintaining a favourable image and consequently a favourable reputation for the company as a whole" which needs to be systematically planned; through managing relevant behaviors, generating communications, and building the symbolism, it will send positive signals to all stakeholders.

Product brands are said to be a direct consequence of a product identification and the strategy of market segmentation (Yu Xie and Boggs 2006). To do product branding, for different products, a company can build separate brand identities; in other words, for a simple company, it may own multiple product brands. Jo Hatch and Schultz (2003) summarized that product brands are mainly created to attract the attention of a limited group of stakeholders (mostly customers) and they are usually of functional importance to the company. The evidence in Leek and Christodoulides' (2011) research indicated that the life cycle of product branding could be comparatively short in some industries. Hence, companies would need to decide whether to use different brands to distinguish different products or to apply a corporate brand as an umbrella that can cover everything (Aaker 2004).

It has been argued that when a product thinking is not fully appreciated, corporate branding may be worth trying, and the company's visibility, recognition, and reputation might be increased, as the corporate branding can reach a greater scale of stakeholders in the past and/or future (Jo Hatch and Schultz 2003). In the study of Jo Hatch and Schultz (2003), both product branding and corporate branding are strategically important, but the corporate branding is concerned more with the company's positioning in its marketplace and creating internal arrangements that help to build up the brand, while the product branding cares more about the functional importance accorded, like marketing and sales. Thus, corporate brands are treated as more significant for it is believed that in that way more well-being can be given to the company (Yu Xie and Boggs 2006).

Branding History of the Company Baoxiniao

Baoxiniao is a garment company, originally registered as "Baoxiniao Holding Ltd." in June 2001, where "Baoxiniao" (in Chinese, "报喜鸟") was retained from its previous brand name used since 1996. The meaning of the name is about "sending good news"; a magpie (also called the "lucky bird") was set as the brand logo, which is regarded as a symbol of auspiciousness in China.

In the 1990s, the development of China's garment industry was in the early stages. At that time, many Chinese people saw the potential of the market; a large number of garment companies were springing up there in the coastal regions—the Zhejiang Province is the most representative one among them. Baoxiniao was founded in Wenzhou, a central city in the southeast of Zhejiang Province, which is famous for its manufacturing industries. The company was established in 1996 through the merging of three local private companies; the professional manager system was introduced to the new business, which distinguished Baoxiniao from most of the local family companies and increased its competitiveness in the national garment industry. The company described the alliance as "an excellent move", which helped Baoxiniao to explore a new way out and laid a solid foundation for the company's success today.

Baoxiniao was awarded the "Wenzhou Famous Brand" in 1997, and further awarded the "Zhejiang Famous Brand" in 1999. These awards were given by the local government to those leading enterprises of good reputation and high productivity. Baoxiniao has attached great importance to product quality since the company was established. At that time, Baoxiniao's main products were men's suits. The company imported the production equipment from Germany and hired skilled experts from Italy to guide their work. In November 1998, the company received the certificate of ISO9001. In order to better serve the Chinese market and prepare for future expansion, Baoxiniao set up a factory in Shanghai and began production in 2000. Since then, Baoxiniao has entered a period of rapid development.

In the last decades, Baoxiniao on the one hand stabilized the domestic market in China; on the other hand, the company was seeking to transform "Baoxiniao" the local brand into an international brand. To pave the way for the international expansion, Baoxiniao renewed the ISO9001 certificate and received another certificate in compliance with ISO14001 in 2002. In July 2003, Baoxiniao signed the contract with a British company Marks & Spencer for suit production and started to access the global market. During 2000–2005, the products of Baoxiniao were no longer limited to men's suits; a new brand BONO was launched by the company in 2000, mainly for the production of business wear for both men and women. Moreover, in order to better fit the international market and make the brand easier to be memorized, the company started using the English brand "Saint Angelo" in 2006, keeping the Chinese brand "报喜鸟" on the logo in the domestic market.

In the development afterward, Baoxiniao procured a series of investments and built their third production base in Hefei, Anhui Province in 2011. The company's annual revenue reached more than five billion. Now Baoxiniao consists of four business units, namely: Phoenix International, Saint Angelo, BONO, and Baoxiniao Venture Investment. Besides Saint Angelo and BONO, the Phoenix International business unit is pretty remarkable. From 2006, the company signed contracts with several international garment companies in Italy and Korea, and Baoxiniao acted as the general agency to introduce these foreign brands into the Chinese market. This co-competitive pattern has lasted throughout the years and continues today. It has been regarded as an important strategy to assist the company in satisfying customers' diverse fashion needs, so that it could focus on the development of their own brands—Saint Angelo and BONO.

Product Brands of Baoxiniao

Up until 2018, there are eleven product brands from Saint Angelo (Picture 2.1), BONO (Picture 2.2), and Phoenix International (Picture 2.3), which are still active in the market.

The business union Saint Angelo now mainly provides medium-to-high-end products and services to satisfy male customers with business professional requirements in their work and daily life. They would like to personally tailor a garment that looks "regal", "elegant", and "exquisite" (features listed on the Saint Angelo's official website) for customers. More than a hundred million RMB was invested into a so-called "Smart Factory" with a system named "Made-To-Measure" (MTM), which was built in 2014 and used in 2015 to obtain relevant data and transfer the data into production. To make the factory work, a large number of employees were hired and trained particularly for the brand. Once a customer generated an order online or offline, Saint Angelo would send a staff member (the company call them the "pattern masters") to collect the basic making data or measure in person. Customers can not only choose the color and the materials used for the garment, but also participate in the garment design and are allowed to monitor the making progress online. A portal of E-MTM is assigned to each customer who requires the service; the customer can check the making progress anytime, as the assembly line is connected to the system and can transmit the data in real-time. Moreover, due to the system being

Picture 2.1 Product brands of Saint Angelo

Picture 2.2 Product brands of BONO

integrated with the logistics system, customers can even acquire delivery information when the garment is ready. The MTM of Saint Angelo was the first trial project of this "one-stop service" in China's garment manufacturing, and they are planning to practice the system in their global markets.

BONO is mainly intended to serve the corporate and customer groups with the requirement of business uniform dress. The "individual tailor" in BONO is not for individual people but more for individual groups with unique characteristics in different industries. They are not only trying to make a smart person but also a smart group. In addition, BONO aims

Picture 2.3 Product brands of Phoenix International

to make their customers look confident, modern, and inspiring, as the appearance of the employees would represent the image of the company. BONO has a design team to study Chinese people's body structure, and living and working habits; BONO tends to make business dresses that are comfortable to wear with excellent quality. So far, the business unit has 80 branches across China, and more than 6000 organizations in the industries of finance, communication, energy, education etc. are customers of BONO.

Phoenix International aims to meet the diversified fashion demands of customers in China by introducing, operating, and expanding international high-end brands from Italy ("TOMBOLINI" and "CAMICISSIMA"), Korea ("HAZZYS"), France ("LAFUMA", is now belong to LG, Korea), and America ("CREMIEUX"); customers can find the brands launched by Phoenix International easily in most shopping malls. Led by Baoxiniao, these brands are actually competing with other high street brands in the Chinese market and have filled the gap of Baoxiniao in the areas of sports and leisure clothing.

Customer Value and Customer-Brand Relationship

Loyal customers can be regarded as key competitive intangible assets (Zhang et al. 2016; Chen 2015). Customer value has been frequently discussed in the context of B2B and B2C marketing (Blocker 2011; Fazal-e-Hasan et al. 2018; Liu et al. 2018), usually defined by the subjective perceptions and evaluations of customers based on their experience of products and/or services (Rintamäki et al. 2007). There are two routes to understand customer value—to invest the assessment of the trade-off between customers' perceived benefits and perceived sacrifices, and to conceptualize the key outcomes of buying (Rintamäki and Kirves 2017). Both of these routes require companies to have the ability to look ahead at what specific customers would value (Zhang et al. 2016) from the on-going relationship (Chen 2015), including what they can offer (their products and services) and the monetary and non-monetary sacrifices to be made in obtaining the benefits they create. To identify competitive customer value propositions, the economic value, functional value, symbolic value, and emotional value are applied as the four most common categories of customer value propositions (Rintamäki and Kirves 2017) to guide relevant strategy making.

Economic value—the monetary worth of an offering to customers (How much the customers would like to pay for the product or service);

Functional value—the perceived utility derived from an offering's capability (What problem this product or service can solve for customers);

Symbolic value—the positive self-attached meanings or good images presented to consumers (How to attract customers and motivate them to think of the products and/or services when needed naturally);

Emotional value—a positive feeling or affective state caused by the functional value or symbolic value (How to generate a good shopping experience for customers).

To Baoxiniao, the economic value and functional value are essential to their business, and the symbolic value and emotional value are also non-negligible. They believe that the company can build and maintain a better relationship with customers only through thinking by point of customers' view and creating larger customer values. In addition, customers would like to pay for products/services with high quality.

> "*We pay attention to the product quality, and we treasure our brands… To be honest, our price is not cheap in the market…*" said the representative of Baoxiniao. For example, trace the price of Saint Angelo online; the lowest price of a "personal tailored shirt" is around 500 RMB (73 US dollar), while the highest could be 3690 RMB (540 US dollars); the lowest price of a "personal tailored garment" is about 2200 RMB (322 US dollar), and the highest price would be definitely more than 10 thousand RMB (1463 US dollar), and the price could even be higher depending on the design and the type of fabric used. However, compared with the brands of the same level in local China, Baoxiniao's product are definitely in a good value in the eyes of the customers.

Competition in the garment industry is increasingly fierce, but the sales of Baoxiniao have actually increased significantly in the past two years after applying the MTM system. Baoxiniao states that the MTM system increased the capability of the "personal tailor" business significantly; it also allows them better communication with customers and helps to further maintain the customer-brand relationship.

In previous research, the customer-brand relationship and brand loyalty have always been discussed together (Hur et al. 2015; Merrilees 2016; Jain et al. 2018), and it has been argued that this relationship could be a long-term one, as related brand consumption is normally derived from a favorable and reliable image of problem-solving in nature. However, the established customer-brand relationship does not mean absolute brand loyalty. Brand loyalty is associated with a deeply held commitment (Samanta 2014) that customers prefer to re-buy a product and/or service currently and in the future. Yeh et al. (2016) pointed out that customer-brand interaction can be fundamental to brand loyalty, and consumption values can be the starters of the relationship (Hur et al. 2015). As the relationship expands, the brand passion and brand trust (Merz et al. 2018) appear; the brand loyalty can be the final outcome of the relationship.

It has been argued that the identity derived by a brand may make the customers feel it matches their actual self, and they may get a strong sense of belongingness (Yeh et al. 2016)—the symbolic value and emotional value in a way take the strategic roles in maintaining the customer-brand relationship.

To obtain the symbolic and emotional value, Baoxiniao even signed two celebrities as the brand ambassadors for the Chinese market. Simon Yam ("任达华"), a Hong Kong actor, was the first brand ambassador of Baoxiniao from 1999; his films are widely known in China, and he was tagged with labels like "gentle", "stylish", and "tough" which are appreciated by Baoxiniao. Many of Baoxiniao's VIP customers even said: "The first time I bought the garment from you is because of Simon Yam… He looks so good in the advertisement!" Baoxiniao quickly sensed the desire of the Chinese male customers—to be a graceful and powerful gentleman. Later, in 2009, Baoxiniao signed another ambassador, Louis Koo ("古天乐"), an actor and singer also from Hong Kong, who is young, but always looks mature and confident. Louis was the idol of the younger generation in China at that time; no matter where he went, it was full of customers. Baoxiniao invited him to attend most of the store opening ceremonies and sponsored many of his shows. The image delivered by Louis is the transition from immaturity to maturity, and it was intended to deliver a message to the consumers—Baoxiniao can help to tailor such a transformation.

"We do encourage customers to take our service and enjoy the shopping experience… whenever you would like to make a change to the product, we would be there to serve", regarded by Baoxiniao. "Customers can also join our VIP club… information of dressing, traveling, and so on are provided regularly which may help our customers to determine their dressing style, and we can further promote our brands at the same time". Due to the popularity of the smartphone and the development of internet technology, convenience and flexibility are increasingly required by the consumers; this is said to be an opportunity for Baoxiniao to systematically manage their customer data and accurately and quickly respond to relevant changing demand. "Customers can enter our online portal on computer or simply with their smart phone"; a portfolio would be made for each of them that contains the figure data, preference data, historic data (purchasing, changing, etc.), and so on. Baoxiniao would like to visualize their interactions to maximize customers' sense of engagement, and thus to build trust.

Strategic Brand Management

Strategic brand management is concerned with sustainability (Erdil 2013), which requires a brand image built on constant favorable evaluations of motivated customers. A brand management system is described as a set of any systems supporting brand-building activities in a firm (Samanta 2014), and the central ideal of a strategic branding expresses the aspiration of top managers for what they will achieve in the future that affects the company (Jo Hatch and Schultz 2003). Yu Xie and Boggs (2006) highlight that it is more than just giving a name to any products or services; it should consider the offering's identification and the strategy of market segmentation. Samanta (2014) argued that in strategic brand management, people tend to over-concentrate on issues of brand building; Liu et al. (2018) proved that the product and brand extensions can also impact a company's profitability and the performance of remaining relevant to customers, the brand leveraging, is one of the important components of strategic brand that needs more attention.

During the early stage of Baoxiniao's development, they committed to a franchise chain with a "consistent image, consistent price, consistent service, and consistent management" ("4-consistent"). Baoxiniao regarded the first five years (1996–2000) as the period of "brand building"; at that time, the strategies for their brand development were: "take quality as the base of the brand", "take design as the soul of the brand", and "take marketing as the life-force of the brand". For the newly created company, the main tasks were to build up the brand "Baoxiniao" and increase brand awareness. Originally, Baoxiniao was built to satisfy customers' requirements of dressing for business occasions. Considering the needs of people of different ages, genders, occupations, and incomes, the brands launched by Baoxiniao subdivided the market and endowed each of them particular features that fit the target customers with various characteristics. The corporate brand wanted to convey a concept of life philosophy, and embody the attitude toward high-quality, fitness, and exquisiteness.

Högström et al. (2015) suggested three strategic brand management archetypes—calculative orientation, heuristic orientation, and dynamic orientation, and they can be differentiated in brand identifying, decision- or strategy- making logic, guiding objective, and time horizon. Under the archetype of calculative orientation, the brand identity refers to the "brand knowledge about the offering", which emphasizes the utilitarian value and extrinsic market value; the decisions or strategies made are to maximize the brand awareness in a short time, where efficiency is the guiding objective. The heuristic orientation stresses the brand meaning and experiences and treasures the symbolic value that aims to match customers' expectations and sociocultural meanings; it requires the maintaining of good market relations in the long term. The dynamic orientation is comparatively a flexible archetype; the brand identity is based on the brand capabilities (extrinsic functional value and symbolic value), the decisions and strategies are to enhance the capabilities that are diversified within the time considered necessary. To optimize the use value of a certain type, companies should carefully evaluate the brand values and the customer values; it is not necessary to stick to one archetype if relevant switching and opportunity costs are acceptable.

To get capital from more diversified sources and further enhance Baoxiniao's impact in the market, in 2001, Baoxiniao opened a venture capital firms. The brand name "Baoxiniao" appeared frequently in various industries including the garment industry. However, it states that the garment business would always be the leading business of Baoxiniao. Baoxiniao sticks to developing their own brands of Saint Angelo and BONO; what is more, it keeps on looking for opportunities to work with good international brands and introduce them to China. In the summer of 2007 (16 August), the company went public. The "Baoxiniao" is becoming a vessel for all product brands that carry them through the wind and waves.

Conclusions

Branding is not only about giving a particular name and image to certain goods and/or services, but also activities to attract consumers and make them always willing to pay for them, which is important throughout any business. If the value of a brand can be well recognized, a lasting customer-brand relationship can be built which would benefit the relevant parties constantly. Baoxiniao, as a local Chinese brand with international ambitions, believes that brand building should come first as a strategic step for a sustainable development. In the context of globalization, there are alternative ways to make business expansion work—taking products in local brands to overseas markets or introducing products to international brands under the umbrella of the corporate brand to local markets. At the current stage, although Baoxiniao's business is mainly in China, in terms of the brand naming and the layout of the four business unions, Baoxiniao is preparing to transform from a Chinese brand into a Chinese international brand.

Further Investigation

1. What brand strategy should Baoxiniao focus on in the Chinese market? The corporate branding or the product branding? Why?
2. If Baoxiniao would like to truly enter the international markets and to become a global brand, what brand strategy should they start with? The corporate branding or the product branding? Why?
3. For Baoxiniao, can you make suggestions for how to further enhance the customer-brand relationship in the context of globalization?

4. Please think of how to develop an Integrated Marketing Communications (IMC) plan for Baoxiniao to realize its ambitions of global branding?
5. What do you think of Baoxiniao's development in the next decade?

References

Aaker, David A. "Leveraging the corporate brand." *California Management Review* 46, no. 3 (2004): 6–18.

Blocker, Christopher P. "Modeling customer value perceptions in cross-cultural business markets." *Journal of Business Research* 64, no. 5 (2011): 533–540.

Chen, Shu-Ching. "Customer value and customer loyalty: Is competition a missing link?" *Journal of Retailing and Consumer Services* 22 (2015): 107–116.

Einwiller, Sabine, and Markus Will. "Towards an integrated approach to corporate branding—An empirical study." *Corporate Communications: An International Journal* 7, no. 2 (2002): 100–109.

Erdil, T. Sabri. "Strategic brand management based on sustainable-oriented view: An evaluation in Turkish home appliance industry." *Procedia-Social and Behavioral Sciences* 99 (2013): 122–132.

Fazal-e-Hasan, Syed Muhammad, Hormoz Ahmadi, Gary Mortimer, Martin Grimmer, and Louise Kelly. "Examining the role of consumer hope in explaining the impact of perceived brand value on customer–brand relationship outcomes in an online retailing environment." *Journal of Retailing and Consumer Services* 41 (2018): 101–111.

Hamin, Hamin, Chris Baumann, and Rosalie L. Tung. "Attenuating double jeopardy of negative country of origin effects and latecomer brand: An application study of ethnocentrism in emerging markets." *Asia Pacific Journal of Marketing and Logistics* 26, no. 1 (2014): 54–77.

Högström, Claes, Anders Gustafsson, and Bård Tronvoll. "Strategic brand management: Archetypes for managing brands through paradoxes." *Journal of Business Research* 68, no. 2 (2015): 391–404.

Hoque, Mohammad Enamul. "MICE destinations branding from corporate branding perspective." *Procedia-Social and Behavioral Sciences* 219 (2016): 307–315.

Hunt, Shelby D. "The ethics of branding, customer-brand relationships, brand-equity strategy, and branding as a societal institution." *Journal of Business Research* 95 (2019): 408–416.

Hur, Won-Moo, Seongho Kang, and Minsung Kim. "The moderating role of Hofstede's cultural dimensions in the customer-brand relationship in China and India." *Cross Cultural Management* 22, no. 3 (2015): 487–508.

Jain, Nikunj Kumar, Shampy Kamboj, Vinod Kumar, and Zillur Rahman. "Examining consumer-brand relationships on social media platforms." *Marketing Intelligence & Planning* 36, no. 1 (2018): 63–78.

Jim Wu, Yen-Chun. "Renaming effect of brand value: State-owned enterprises." *Management Decision* 47, no. 10 (2009): 1555–1581.

Jo Hatch, Mary, and Majken Schultz. "Bringing the corporation into corporate branding." *European Journal of Marketing* 37, no. 7/8 (2003): 1041–1064.

Leek, Sheena, and George Christodoulides. "A literature review and future agenda for B2B branding: Challenges of branding in a B2B context." *Industrial Marketing Management* 40, no. 6 (2011): 830–837.

Laforet, Sylvie, and Junsong Chen. "Chinese and British consumers' evaluation of Chinese and international brands and factors affecting their choice." *Journal of World Business* 47, no. 1 (2012): 54–63.

Li, Hung-Hui, Min-Yu Hsieh, and William Li Chang. "Lucky names: Superstitious beliefs in Chinese corporate branding strategy for bank marketing." *The North American Journal of Economics and Finance* 35 (2016): 226–233.

Liu, Yeyi, Thomas Foscht, Andreas B. Eisingerich, and Huei-Ting Tsai. "Strategic management of product and brand extensions: Extending corporate brands in B2B vs. B2C markets." *Industrial Marketing Management* 71 (2018): 147–159.

Merrilees, Bill. "Interactive brand experience pathways to customer-brand engagement and value co-creation." *Journal of Product & Brand Management* 25, no. 5 (2016): 402–408.

Merz, Michael A., Lia Zarantonello, and Silvia Grappi. "How valuable are your customers in the brand value co-creation process? The development of a customer co-creation value (CCCV) scale." *Journal of Business Research* 82 (2018): 79–89.

Murphy, Judy. "Branding." *Marketing Intelligence & Planning*, 6, no. 4 (1988): 4–8.

Rintamäki, Timo, Hannu Kuusela, and Lasse Mitronen. "Identifying competitive customer value propositions in retailing." *Managing Service Quality: An International Journal* 17, no. 6 (2007): 621–634.

Rintamäki, Timo, and Kaisa Kirves. "From perceptions to propositions: Profiling customer value across retail contexts." *Journal of Retailing and Consumer Services* 37 (2017): 159–167.

Samanta, Irene, ed. *Strategic marketing in fragile economic conditions*. Hershey, PA: IGI Global, 2014. https://doi.org/10.4018/978-1-4666-6232-2.

Schaefer, Anja. "Consumer knowledge and country of origin effects." *European Journal of Marketing* 31, no. 1 (1997): 56–72.

Silva, Rosario, Oksana Gerwe, and Manuel Becerra. "Corporate brand and hotel performance: A resource-based perspective." *Journal of Business Research* 79 (2017): 23–30.

Steenkamp, Jan-Benedict. "How global brands create firm value: The 4 V model." *International Marketing Review* 31, no. 1 (2014): 5–29.

Tarnovskaya, Veronika, Ulf Elg, and Steve Burt. "The role of corporate branding in a market driving strategy." *International Journal of Retail & Distribution Management* 36, no. 11 (2008): 941–965.

Vallaster, Christine, and Adam Lindgreen. "Corporate brand strategy formation: Brand actors and the situational context for a business-to-business brand." *Industrial Marketing Management* 40, no. 7 (2011): 1133–1143

Voss, Kevin E., and Mayoor Mohan. "Corporate brand effects in brand alliances." *Journal of Business Research* 69, no. 10 (2016): 4177–4184.

Yeh, Ching-Hsuan, Yi-Shun Wang, and Kaili Yieh. "Predicting smartphone brand loyalty: Consumer value and consumer-brand identification perspectives." *International Journal of Information Management* 36, no. 3 (2016): 245–257.

Yu Xie, Henry, and David J. Boggs. "Corporate branding versus product branding in emerging markets: A conceptual framework." *Marketing Intelligence & Planning* 24, no. 4 (2006): 347–364.

Zhang, Hao, Xiaoning Liang, and Shiquan Wang. "Customer value anticipation, product innovativeness, and customer lifetime value: The moderating role of advertising strategy." *Journal of Business Research* 69, no. 9 (2016): 3725–3730.

CHAPTER 3

From No Body to Some Body: A Resource Based View Approach for the Branding of a Manufacturer

Paul C. Y. Liu, Fei Zhu and Jie Wang

Introduction

Both retail and industrial firms strive for brand awareness and recognition in the marketplace. Advertising, TV commercials, and/or social media just "social media" or "going viral on social media" don't seem applicable for industrial manufacturers. It is obvious that retail and industrial firms have different strategic marketing approaches. In our observations, collaborating and affiliating might be common strategic marketing practices for small and medium industrial manufacturers. Affiliating with industry leaders by collaboration could be one of the initial steps to take. Collaborations

P. C. Y. Liu (✉) · F. Zhu · J. Wang
Nottingham University Business School China, Ningbo, China
e-mail: chingyuanpaul.liu@nottingham.edu.cn

F. Zhu
e-mail: fei.zhu@nottingham.edu.cn

J. Wang
e-mail: jie.wang@nottingham.edu.cn

M. J. Liu and J. Luo (eds.), *China Branding*,
https://doi.org/10.1007/978-981-13-9318-1_3

bring new values (Peters et al. 2010a, b) to small manufacturers who can focus on resources, maximizing production efficiencies, minimizing production costs, being part of the industry knowledge network, enhancing their competencies, and promoting its brand recognition in the marketplace, while their world-class partners enjoy minimized production cost, leveraged R&D expenditures, and shared supply chain risks etc. It works in an equal interlocking and interactive formation for both those in collaboration; however, the small manufacturers may benefit more from it, particularly, resource mixture and reallocation, brand affiliations, and Word-of-Mouth effects. In the past decades, we have seen Japanese SMBs evolved and transformed into world-class competitors from strategic collaborations with industry leading American firms. Likewise, Chinese SMBs are collaborating with Western industry leading original equipment manufacturer (OEMs) for growth.

This case study is concerned with how a small local Zhejiang gear manufacturer, Shuang Huan Company (SHC), grew, rose, and built its brand recognition via exploring and exploiting resources obtained from collaborations with world-class partners. The intertwined strategy used several strategic tactics to achieve its development and branding goals. SHC was a medium-sized, private gear supplier, who had collaborated with global OEMs, such as ZF and John Deere from 2005. The collaborations had provided opportunities that allowed SHC's name to appear alongside those world-class well-known international partners. It also required SHC to seek higher standards for product quality, better managerial methods, and more profound development scopes, which all contributed to its branding. While receiving more advanced skills, sophisticated knowledge, and information from the collaborators, SHC got to engage in higher production standards and better managerial methods building its competitive advantages and bringing positive reputation naturally in the marketplace. SHC has been able to improve its resources possessing VIRN (Valuable, Rare, Imperfectly inimitable and Non-substitutable) attributes serving both domestic and international customers efficiently and effectively while differentiating from the rest of the thousands of gear manufacturers in the competitive Chinese gear industry. Resource-Based View is used to explain the phenomena observed in SHC. From an RBV standpoint, the interlocking and interactive implementation of strategic tactics, i.e. brand affiliation, word-of-mouth effect, collaboration etc., that SHC took have joined forces together in building SHC's brand (see Fig. 3.1) and created barriers to competitors both domestically and internationally.

Fig. 3.1 Connection between 5 factors

Literature

Resource Based View

Resource-based view is based on the concept of economic rent and the view of the firm as a collection of capabilities (Barney 1991). A resource can be considered as something that could bring advantages or disadvantages to a given firm (Wernerfelt 1984), or valuable assets that enable the firm to conceive and implement strategies that improve its efficiency and effectiveness (Barney 2001). Furthermore, firms explore and exploit resources to be VRIN to gain their competitive advantages. Valuable is when a particular resource contributes to a given firm's competitive advantage. Rare is when a resource is obtained that can't be easily found by competitors. An inimitable resource is one that cannot be replicated by competitors. A non-substitutable resource is a resource that cannot be replaced in building competitive advantage. According to Barney and Clark (2007), firms either mix resources they possess, acquire externally, or that are embedded within firms internally for VRIN resources to gain competitive advantages. Furthermore, Porter (1985) asserts that firms gain competitive advantages through cost reduction and differentiation to create barriers for competitors. As such, having partners with established brands may be considered as a resource that firms are able to explore and exploit into VRIN resources by focusing on improving a specific set of skills and knowledge in production, increasing efficiency, reducing the costs, enhancing innovative capabilities, and differentiating its brand by affiliating itself with well-known collaboration partners.

Brand Affiliation

Before it is to be known in the market, to be seen could be the first step for small manufacturers. Putting their own names alongside well-known partners through collaboration might be one of the methods to accomplish this. Conventional industrial marketing tactics, such as joining trade shows and cold-visiting customers can only help small manufacturers to present to and perhaps help their prospective customers to know what they do, or merely to know who they are. In order to gain further credibility and trust, knowing what they do helps little to earn customers. Instead, it may be more important to let prospective customers know who their partners are. Brand Affiliation certainly brings strong endorsements, not only to be known for the things they do best, but also for small manufacturers to benefit from the things their partners do best. In other words, brand affiliation portrays extended images of certain capabilities and qualities the small manufacturers and their partners possess. Extending their brands in affiliation with well-known, world-class partners may attract more clients to become alternative sources of revenue. Recognition of superior quality requirements further enhances the word-of-mouth within the industry as product quality speaks for itself; one of the key components to strengthen or augment brand attributes to further differentiate from competitors. Governments also can be strong brands. Firms enhance further brand differentiation from collaborating and affiliating with governments. Firms may be involved in enacting industry standards, joining particular projects, or being chosen to promote its creditability and recognition within the industry. Such affiliation also brings and increases brand equity for firms to differentiate themselves. To sum up, brand affiliations allow smaller firms to establish and differentiate their brands from others.

Collaboration

Collaboration is defined as the process of organizations working together to complete a task or achieve a goal (Marinez-Moyano 2006). It comes in forms, such as joint ventures, outsourcing arrangements, product licensing, cooperative research, or strategic alliances. Vendors, OEMs, and suppliers often form collaborations in a supply chain, where firms work together to achieve greater competitive advantages in supply chain operations (Cao and Zhang 2011) in order to compete (Togar and Ramaswami 2008). Whether to reduce the production cost, or share R&D expenditures and warranty risks, such vertical collaboration in the supply chain allows OEMs to share information and resources with suppliers who are then able to concentrate on production resources for higher quality and lower costs for better competitiveness (Cao et al. 2010). Also, OEMs and suppliers might share market information and joint knowledge creation to expedite innovative response and reduce R&D expenditure collectively (Malhotra et al. 2005). Small suppliers often benefit more from obtaining resources and capabilities to enhance their brand's awareness in associating with world-class brands. For example, vertical supply chain collaboration is a usual practice that a vendor, OEMs, and suppliers jointly undertake to serve end buyers in the automobile industry, in particular, automakers, whose brand reputation depends on the quality of assembly and production of OEMs and suppliers. At the same time, they tend to push the responsibilities, risks, and margins downward to their supply chains (Chatterjee et al. 2002) due to the market demand for new models with a shorter turnaround time frame, more competitive pricing, and higher quality measurements. OEMs and suppliers are working together closely to strive for survival; information, resources, investments, responsibilities, risks, and efforts are shared.

Word-of-Mouth

As mentioned above, brand affiliation might be one of the ways to establish new clients in industrial marketing and so too is word-of-mouth. For firms, especially, whose sales are derived from mostly face-to-face relationships, word-of-mouth is extremely important. It shares the concept with referrals from ancient times where recommendations, testimonials, and celebrity effects are commonly seen in retail and industry. Word-of-mouth, reputation, or branding are similar tactics to be used in manufacturing. Despite whom you work with, this referral requires your partners of suppliers to speak positively about the supplier rather than it bluffing itself. This may only happen when the customers are happy. OEMs might be pleased when superior quality products and exceptional services are offered from the supplier and they would be more than happy to give out positive comments regarding the supplier. It is particularly important for small manufacturers because positive referrals from prominent OEMs might represent new opportunities for alternative sources of revenue. In addition, government endorsements are another form of word-of-mouth, which is particularly important in China. Awards, research grants, and/or an opportunity to join enacting industrial standards are significant representations and confirmations for small manufacturers to differentiate themselves from their domestic competitors. To sum up, when the word spreads across the industry, brand awareness and recognition increase and further aids differentiation.

Chinese Gear Industry

Since the 1980s SHC was one of the gear manufacturers competing in low value-added motorcycle parts among thousands of competitors. Under the support of government policies, the Chinese gear industry has transited from low-end products to high value-added products throughout the past 30 years. The entire industry has enjoyed an 18% annual growth rate for the first 10 years. Initially, mass production of motorcycles has boosted the industry growth to RMB 20 billion annually. It developed with the increasing demand of car gear components after the motorcycle rush and took off to an RMB 130 billion industry in the following 10 years. In the past decade, the industry enjoyed a growth of 230 billion annual sales due to the increase in green technology, an innovation of windmill generators, and precision industrial gears. However, since 3 years ago, the entire industry has suffered a stagnant period of time. This is partly due to most Chinese gear manufacturers still producing low-end, low price products. Their main competition is to offer cheap products, cheaper than their competitors, with no branding consciousness. The increase of low-end competitors from developing countries has hit the industry and the trading deficit has widened. Only a few companies, whose annual sales have exceeded RMB 100 million, and who have started to recognize the issue of branding, have been the exception. SHC is one of them.

Shuang Huan Company

Following the explosive growth of the Chinese gear industry, SHC also grew in this golden era. However, SHC was still a no brand, mediocre company supplying motorcycle gear, which was established in 1980 with an initial investment of RMB 3000. By the year 2001, SHC was a fourth tier gear producer, small and unknown, in the industry. With more open market competition when China joined the WTO, the founder realized the importance of differentiating themselves from their fellow competitors. Instead of continuing to compete on prices, SHC determined to establish its reputation in the industry through its quality products.

Establishing Collaborations

In 2005, four years after the internationalization and liberalization of China joining the WTO, SHC also opened up the opportunity of collaborating with Zahnradfabrik Friedrichshafen AG (ZF), a German world-class automobile gear parts and drivetrain OEM. In 2006, SHC further collaborated with John Deere, a U.S. leading manufacturer of agricultural, construction, and forestry machinery. In the following years, SHC collaborated with more than fifteen fortunate 500 companies in various industries, for example, BorgWarner, DANA, DEMAG and FIAT in the automobile industry, Black & Decker and Bosch in the power tool industry, and RV gears etc. Another collaboration for SHC was to work with governments to set industry standards. Both the governments and firms work together in raising the bar of the industry standards for quality purposes. SHC was invited to be involved in erecting higher standards and setting the production process as the leader of the gear industry. Apart from its experience and knowledge from their international collaborations, SHC further differentiates from its competitors and enjoys a great leap in regulations from its competitive advantages, not to mention the representation and the image of being the leader of the industry. Collaborations work in a positive circle of improvement. That is, the closer the collaboration relationships are, the stronger the SHC will be. Relationships in the supply chain create an inimitable and non-substitutable resource for SHC.

Applying Resource-Based View

The collaborations did not only bring pay cheques to SHC but also VRIN resources, for example, market information and advanced knowledge to help upgrading its production capability, including process, machinery, materials, and managerial systems to meet their production standards and increase their competitiveness. According to SHC, ZF, and John Deere had initially sent their professionals to SHC for guiding and consulting purposes, to satisfy their requirements for production. Quickly exploring and exploiting the resources obtained from the collaborations, SHC gradually established and held its competitive ground. SHC also accumulated experience, knowledge, and information on the basis of production and future innovation. The in-house research and development subsidiary and collaborations with universities were established in 2010 to support and serve the demands of clients. Through involving partners in the development process, SHC does not only contribute to its expertise regarding gears but also receives up-to-date industry information. From the collaborations with universities, SHC does not only assist its clients for better R&D capability, it helps to reduce the costs along the supply chain and also gain cutting-edge technologies. In addition, innovative experiences also contribute to its outstanding innovative services to all other clients in general. Furthermore, innovation does not stop at the technologic level; SHC also creatively introduced several managerial innovative mechanisms while striving to meet clients' production requirements. Hence, VRIN resources are formed. In addition, in 2008, the introduction of Toyota Production System (TPS) for quality improvements, particularly Kaizen, the concept of continuous improvement, has led SHC to fortify its competitive advantage by exploring and mixing resources. The use of the core concept of Kaizen helps SHC to continuously improve product quality, production process, managerial system, and employee works. SHC invites professionals (to explore new resources) from Toyota to introduce and implement (exploit) TPS, a complete transformation of the mind-set of the entire company. With these strong collaborations, SHC has gone IPO in the Shenzhen Stock Exchange in 2010, which helps firms to grow even stronger and further differentiate itself due to the strong financial support (explore new resources) from the financial market. Ever since, with the purchase of cutting-edge production machinery and tools (exploit), SHC has grown from a no-name gear producer to a well-branded international gear supplier and generated RMN 400 million in annual sales in 35 years. SHC also utilized the knowledge, information, and resources gained from the collaborations and financial market to form VRIN resources to fortify its collaborations as well as differentiate its brand. As Dyer (1996) asserts that relation-specific investment often results in superior performance, SHC is able to concentrate on productions, and to continue exploring, exploiting, and developing resources into VRIN resources for its strategic goals. SHC invests heavily not only in tools and machinery but also management systems and human resources which result in a combination of superior products and service qualities which in turn lead to a good reputation and positive word-of-mouth, which helps to upgrade its brand recognition and contribute to the formation of increased and stronger collaborations.

Affiliating with Well-Known Brands

The amazing achievement of SHC, who profits and gains production and innovation capabilities from collaborating with world-class firms like ZF, John Deere, BrogWanner, Bosch, Fiat, Ford, etc. while affiliating its brand with these firms, also requires SHC to increase its capabilities in order to keep up with them. An old saying in China which was brought up in the interview with the Minister of Operations of SHC is "Bang Da Kuan, Xue Xian Jin." "Bang (be with) Da (big) Kuan (an individual or organization)" means to be with/collaborate with partners who have advanced production skills, greater financial resources, greater branding power, and so on. Being with companies like ZF, John Deere, and ABB, etc. certainly fulfills this aim of being associated with brand names in the industry. "Xue" (to learn from) "Xian Jin" (a superior individual or organization who represents certain sectors) means to obtain advanced technology, managerial tools, and marketing concepts from leading organizations in the industry. As well as the information, knowledge, and skills learnt from collaborating with those international OEMs, SHC has also learnt to improve its production process from TPS of Toyota. With the import of a computerized ERP system, robotic automation, and a reformed production process to minimize waste, including material, rate of defects, and time of production (Just-in-time), the purchase of automation and precision manufacturing tools, the introduction of components shops and production tickets (from TPS), SHC has reduced production costs, increased its revenue, elevated the product quality, and earned its reputation of delivering quality products on time. Although it was not officially confirmed, SHC followed this strategy deliberately taking the route of internationalization; of collaborating with other global OEMs to obtain market information and advanced knowledge for production capabilities and differentiated recognition of its brand.

Building Word of Mouth

The successful import of TPS has helped SHC reach superior product quality and to win a positive reputation in the industry with more collaboration with global partners, like ABB, Magna, Cummings, Yamaha, and Volvo as well as some domestic giants, like SAIC Motor, SINOTruk, and BYD. With the innovative power, outstanding customer support, and superior quality gear products, SHC does not only meet the production prerequisites from its international partners, and earn its reputation among domestic clients, but also differentiates its brand further away from its competitors. The result from improved product quality throughout the years has brought SHC recognition from governments and rendered awards to manifest the great achievements of the company. In addition, offering superior service to customers is another key to differentiate itself. SHC offers on-site engineering support for a quick response to the demand of its OEM clients in the collaborations. By providing close customer service and support, SHC does not only fortify the already tight relationships with exceptional customer satisfaction and positive branding, but government awards also bring brand recognition domestically. SHC has earned national awards, e.g. National High-tech R&D Award (863 Program) from The Ministry of Science and Technology, 2015 Intelligent Manufacturing Program from Ministry of Industry and Information Technology, National certified High-tech Center from National Development and Reform Commission, Ministry of science and technology, Ministry of Finance, General Administration of Customs and State Administration of Taxation etc. SHC have also won provincial awards, such as ZhejiangMade from the Zhejiang provincial Government, Zhejiang Key Enterprises Research Center from the Zhejiang Provincial Government, Award for innovation of enterprise management in Zhejiang from the Zhejiang Provincial Economy and Information Commission, and municipality awards, such as the 2014 Annual Model Enterprise of Innovation and Transformation from the Taizhou Municipal Government etc. These awards help SHC to establish a positive word of mouth effect among its Chinese producers, clients, and governments, which is a significant recognition in China. Despite creating happy customers with its superior products and service quality, SHC has an additional unique way of managing its own reputation, that is, a zero lawsuit policy, which has become a story told among the Chinese gear industry and international OEMs. When these stories are dispersed and told, a legend of a brand then appears.

Managerial Implications

In the case of SHC, there is a clear pathway of how a small company grows through integrating resources in collaborations to form barriers. As Hamel et al. (1989) state, collaboration is a low-cost route for small suppliers to gain technology and market access. Such long-term and close arrangements do not only reduce the cost of production, innovation, and transaction costs, but also reduce the risks of development and quality assurance for the parties involved. By applying the RBV and collaborative strategy, the small suppliers can focus on growing their core offerings to reduce the production costs (partially due to increasing the volume of material purchased and partially due to decreasing the amount of waste of material and time), improve product quality, and build its brand to differentiate from the competition. The successful path of SHC leads to the question of how firms apply RBV and applicable strategies for their long-term competitiveness. Indeed, who to collaborate with may be important; however, it is also crucial to preserve and utilize the resources gained from the collaboration and transform into VRIN types for competitive advantages. SHC has won the opportunities to collaborate with world-class OEMs and automakers initially; it has also introduced mechanisms to transform in order to stay in the collaborations.

Conclusion and Discussion

To sum up, other small suppliers in China can learn from the experience of SHC. The intertwined strategic planning combines resource exploration and exploitation, collaboration with global partners, brand affiliation, and word-of-mouth tactics. The specific knowledge, information, skills, resources, innovations resources, and relationships brought to SHC build strong competitive advantages and enable the brand to compete with others. SHC seized the moment and strategized to explore and exploit the resources obtained, by utilizing the resources to form a barrier from enhanced and improved production and innovation capabilities, and superior product quality, to capture the effects of word-of-mouth and brand affiliation to fortify the collaborative relationship and enhanced brand recognition which are the key factors to grow and compete. Further in the case study, SHC introduced TPS to respond to clients' demands of quality products. Subconsciously, the tactics helped SHC to quickly establish its branding as the leading role in the Chinese gear industry. However, SHC's revenue is still heavily dependent upon the collaboration in the supply chain in the automobile industry. Even though the transaction costs may seem high, the fear of being replaced in the network is still like the Sword of Damocles. Quickly utilizing the resources and branding to diverse its dependency on the automobile collaboration network may be the next step for SHC to seek.

Further Investigation

1. How did SHC build its brand? What strategic approach did it use?
2. Identify strategy or strategies SHC used.
3. Identify the strategic goal and how SHC achieved it.

References

Barney, Jay. "Firm resources and sustained competitive advantage." *Journal of Management* 17, no. 1 (1991): 99–120.

Barney, Jay B. "Resource-based theories of competitive advantage: A ten-year retrospective on the resource-based view." *Journal of Management* 27, no. 6 (2001): 643–650.

Barney, Jay B., and Delwyn N. Clark. *Resource-based theory: Creating and sustaining competitive advantage.* Oxford University Press on Demand from Google Scholar, 2007.

Cao, Mei, Mark A. Vonderembse, Qingyu Zhang, and T. S. Ragu-Nathan. "Supply chain collaboration: Conceptualisation and instrument development." *International Journal of Production Research* 48, no. 22 (2010): 6613–6635.

Cao, Mei, and Qingyu Zhang. "Supply chain collaboration: Impact on collaborative advantage and firm performance." *Journal of Operations Management* 29, no. 3 (2011): 163–180.

Chatterjee, A., A. Satpathy, N. Ganguli, and T. V. Kumaresh. "Collaboration: Key to world-class quality." *Quality* 41, no. 6 (2002): 50–53.

Dyer, Jeffrey H. "Specialized supplier networks as a source of competitive advantage: Evidence from the auto industry." *Strategic Management Journal* 17, no. 4 (1996): 271–291.

Hamel, Gary, Yves L. Doz, and Coimbatore K. Prahalad. "Collaborate with your competitors and win." *Harvard Business Review* 67, no. 1 (1989): 133–139.

Martinez-Moyano, I. "Exploring the dynamics of collaboration in interorganizational settings." In *Creating a culture of collaboration: The International Association of Facilitators handbook*, 69. Vol. 4. San Francisco, CA: Jossey-Bass, A Wiley Imprint, 2006.

Malhotra, Arvind, Sanjay Gosain, and Omar A. El Sawy. "Absorptive capacity configurations in supply chains: Gearing for partner-enabled market knowledge creation." *MIS Quarterly* 29, no. 1 (2005, March): 145–187. 2 Diagrams, 12 Charts.

Peters, L. D., A. D. Pressey, W. J. Johnston, and T. Kendrick. "Collaboration and collective learning: Networks as learning organisations." *Journal of Business & Industrial Marketing* 25, no. 6 (2010a): 478–484.

Peters, M. J. L., D. P. M. Symmons, D. McCarey, B. A. C. Dijkmans, P. Nicola, T. K. Kvien, I. B. McInnes, et al. "EULAR evidence-based recommendations for cardiovascular risk management in patients with rheumatoid arthritis and other forms of inflammatory arthritis." *Annals of the Rheumatic Diseases* 69, no. 2 (2010b): 325–331.

Porter, Michael E. *Competitive advantage: Creating and sustaining superior performance*. New York: Free Press, 1985.

Simatupang, Togar M., and Ramaswami Sridharan. "Design for supply chain collaboration." *Business Process Management Journal* 14, no. 3 (2008): 401–418.

Wernerfelt, Birger. "A resource-based view of the firm." *Strategic Management Journal* 5, no. 2 (1984): 171–180.

CHAPTER 4

Innovation in Environmental Technologies in China: The Case of Feida's Power Plant Pollution Control Equipment

Peter S. Hofman, Chenchen Weng, Steven Shijin Zhou and Abby Jingzi Zhou

Introduction

The availability of electricity plays a pivotal role in China's economic development and much of its electricity has been produced by coal-fired power plants. In the past decades between 70% and 80% of the electricity generated in China was based on coal (Yuan et al. 2018). Alongside the benefits of coal-fired power generation, there are significant negative side-effects. They include air emissions which can lead to increased local air pollution and contribute to climate change. In recent years the focus has shifted from ensuring that economic growth can be facilitated by electricity generation to a more sustainable growth based on cleaner and greener electricity generation (NEA 2016; Lin 2017). For coal-fired power generation, this has triggered an increasing use of counter-acting measures to reduce air emis-

P. S. Hofman (✉) · C. Weng · S. S. Zhou · A. J. Zhou
University of Nottingham Ningbo China, Ningbo, China
e-mail: peter.hofman@nottingham.edu.cn

M. J. Liu and J. Luo (eds.), *China Branding*,
https://doi.org/10.1007/978-981-13-9318-1_4

sions and their harmful impacts, globally as well as in China (Metz et al. 2001; Hofman 2005; NEA 2016; Lin 2017). In the global industry for pollution control systems for power plants, China is playing an important role given its strong demand for pollution control equipment for coal-fired power stations. One of the leading companies in pollution control equipment for thermal power plants in China is Zhejiang Feida Environmental Science & Technology Co. Ltd. (in short: Feida).[1] This chapter will analyze and evaluate the case of Feida in more detail and focus on the following questions:

- What have been the major milestones and accomplishments in the development of Feida?
- What role did research and development (R&D) and innovation play in enabling Feida to become a market leader and well-known domestic brand?
- To what extent can the company be considered as a global leader and why?

The chapter will continue with a short introduction of the history of Feida, followed by a more detailed analysis of innovation in Feida and its role in brand building. Consequently, we will focus on the international position of Feida and compare Feida's strategy and innovation with a leading global player. We end with some recommendations and a number of questions that could be central to a teaching case on strategy and innovation in emerging market firms.

Feida's Development

Feida was founded in 1969 in the Zhejiang Province in China. Figure 4.1 demonstrates milestones in the company's development from 1969 to 2016. Feida has specialized in power plant emission control systems from the 1980s, and set up a research institute on electrostatic precipitators (ESPs) with the help of the UN development program. ESPs can remove fine dust and small particles from gases and smoke and are widely used in power plants that use coal. Feida became a leading firm domestically in ESPs and broader environmental technologies and received the title of national

[1] See the website of Feida at https://www.feidaep.com/En.

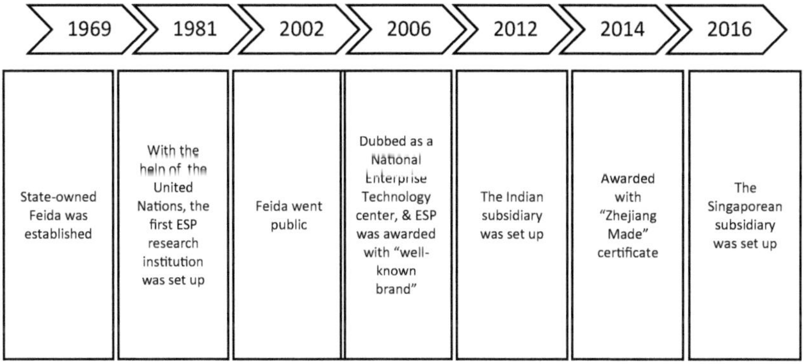

Fig. 4.1 Company history

flagship enterprise and Equipment Manufacturing Base for Environmental Protection Machinery because of its solid performance and good reputation. Feida has also been awarded as a High-Tech Enterprise by the Central Government of China and is recognized as a "ZhejiangMade" brand by the Zhejiang Provincial Administration for Market Regulation. Feida was named as "Pilot Enterprise of Environment Protection" by the United Nations Environment Program for their contribution toward environmental protection in China in 2011.

The firm provides a series of products, including ESPs, flue gas desulphurization equipment, fabric filters, pneumatic conveyor equipment, hazardous solid waste treatment equipment, and electrical control equipment. It also provides technical guidance and installation services both in China and outside of China. Picture 4.1 gives an example of Feida's products. The 600 MW power plant was built by the China Huaneng Group. It was one of the first power plants that used localized ultra-supercritical ESP technology provided by Feida in 2002.

The Connection Between Innovation and Branding

Various studies have identified and confirmed the significant influence of innovation on brand performance (Agarwal et al. 2003; Beverland et al. 2010). In fact, the most well-known companies in the world are often also at the forefront of innovation; consider, for example, firms like Apple, Siemens, General Electric, Unilever, Volkswagen, Bosch, Alibaba, Alstom,

Picture 4.1 Qinbei Power Plant in Jiyuan City, Henan Province, China

and so forth. There are also many well-known brands from Asian companies such as Toyota, Honda, Samsung, and Hyundai, whose success has been a combination of providing quality and value for money next to innovation strength (Kapferer 2012). In a well-known textbook on strategic brand management, it is mentioned that innovation is like "oxygen" for a company's brand (Kapferer 2012, p. 202). A steady flow of innovation may be necessary to remain attractive to customers; this can be a range of incremental innovations or every now and then a new business model or pioneering innovation, depending on the industry in which the firm is active (Srinivasan et al. 2009). In a competitive industry environment, a company's internal learning ability is critical for its innovation capabilities and innovation output, and the significance of its innovation output influences the company's reputation and brand performance (Weerawardena et al. 2006). Apart from internal sources and capabilities for innovation, it is well established that the nature of innovation in firms is also connected

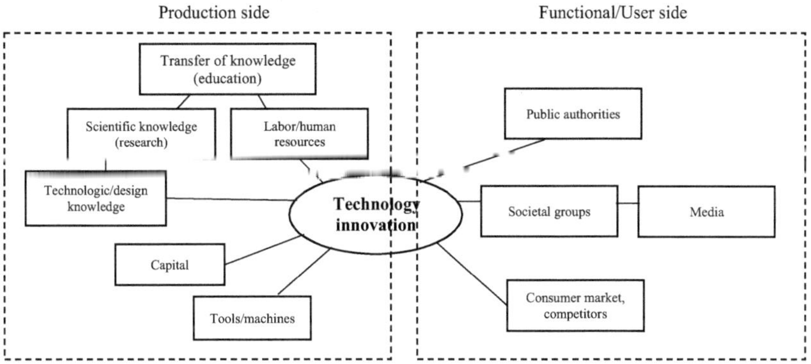

Fig. 4.2 Elements of firm-level innovation system practices

with the context in which it operates which can be represented by a broader innovation system. "The capability of a firm to innovate is therefore not solely determined by internal factors, such as its strategy, culture and organization, but also by the nature of a firm's interaction with external actors, such as knowledge institutes, government organizations, users and capital providers" (Hofman and de Bruijn 2010, p. 116) and institutions such as regulators of the electricity sector and power plants as in the case of Feida. These interactions are shaped to some extent by firms themselves, but also significantly by the nature of the innovation system in which they operate. This innovation system shapes the direction of innovation and consists of various actor groups that are connected to the production, use, and function of the innovation practices. Figure 4.2, based on Geels (2004), illustrates the various actor groups involved in innovation systems. From the perspective of the production side, the firm-level innovative practices could be influenced by scientific knowledge (e.g. universities, public and private laboratories), capital (e.g. venture capital suppliers, banks, insurance firms), technologic/design knowledge (e.g. design firms, technical institutes, consultancies), transfer of knowledge (e.g. school, universities), labor/human resources (e.g. laborers, skilled personnel), tools/machines (e.g. suppliers of materials, components, tools). For the functional/user side, the innovation system approaches could also be affected by the factors of public authorities (e.g. government), societal groups (e.g. NGOs), consumers, and media (e.g. TV, newspapers, magazines).

Our description and analysis of Feida will be embedded within the context of this innovation system. The purpose is to understand what key actors and institutions influence Feida's innovation, analyze to what extent Feida is connected to the most advanced innovation actors related to emission control of power plants (such as knowledge institutes, research centers, and other companies), and assess how Feida could further advance its innovation as well as its branding.

Technology Innovation at Feida

Technology innovation has been one of the main elements of the company's strategy. Through a continuous emphasis on research and development (R&D) and innovation, the company has been distinguished as a leading innovation company in the power generation sector and environmental technology industry in China. Within China, Feida has more than 50 domestic patents of original innovation and secondary innovation, and the company received around 60 prizes for its technologic progress.[2] As chair of the Machinery Division of the National Environment-protection Institute of Standardization in China, Feida has played a leading role in drafting 14 documents of national standards, and 103 files of industrial standards.

Table 4.1 presents some of the most important research projects at Feida. Feida does not only focus on new product innovations but also invests in research on process innovations, e.g. approaches to lower the production costs of emission control systems, enhancing the efficiency of dust removal systems, and enhancing the operational reliability and stability of power plants and their emission control systems. Picture 4.2 shows the Sanhe power plant that was built by the Guohua Electric Power Group in 2015. Feida provided wet ESP for one of the 300 MW units. The dust density reached 0.41 mg/m^3, which set a new world record of the lowest dust emission of a coal-fired power plant. It is one of the three "Energy Conservation and Emission Reduction Demonstration Power Plants" in China.

[2] Secondary innovation in China refers to innovations developed by companies through importing advanced technology from abroad, and adjusting it for the Chinese market.

Table 4.1 Key research projects at Feida

No.	*Project*	*Project category*	*Year*	*Funding (million RMB)*	*Source of funding*	*Collaborators*
1	Big coal-fired plant boiler smoke elec-bag dust-remover technology and equipment	863 plan	2007–2010	28.04	National funding: 4.73 Local funding: 1.15 Feida: 22.16	Zhejiang University; Northeastern University
2	Technology and equipment for PM2.5 collector at coal-fired plant	863 plan	2013–2015	14.61	National funding: 4.08 Feida: 6.42	Zhejiang University
3	PM2.5 collection based on the technology of electrocoagulation and new type power supply	Zhejiang key research project	2008–2012	7.13	Provincial funding: 0.71 Feida: 6.42	Zhejiang University
4	High-ash coal and low technology and its application	National key research plan	2016–2020	Budget 12.06	National funding: 4.39 Feida: 7.67	Zhejiang University; Shanghai University of Electric Power; Huadian Electric Power; Zhejiang Hope Environmental Protection Engineering Co. Ltd

(continued)

Table 4.1 (continued)

No.	*Project*	*Project category*	*Year*	*Funding (million RMB)*	*Source of funding*	*Collaborators*
5	Air protection innovation base	National key research plan	2016–2019	Budget 13.25	National funding: 5.25 Feida: 8	/
6	New high-efficiency electrostatic precipitators	National key research plan	2017–2020	Budget 22.70	National funding: 5.2 Feida: 17.50	Shandong University; University of Nottingham, Ningbo, China; China Power Engineering Consulting Group; University of Science and Technology Beijing

Picture 4.2 Sanhe Power Plant, Sanhe City, Hebei Province, China

Technology Innovation Strategy

A continuous focus on technologic innovation is critical for Feida to maintain its leading position in the industry. Generally, the evolution of technology in Feida has been driven by three main factors, namely the needs of the market, the internal capabilities and strategy of Feida, and its links to international leading companies (Wu et al. 2001). Figure 4.3 shows the evolution of Feida's technologic innovation strategy. Feida firstly developed its own products by relying on its own technology and resources. After the development of this first-generation product, Feida has kept on improving the performance of the product through careful analysis of customers' feedback and by reducing the gap between their product and the products provided by leading international competitors. One of the pathways Feida has used to improve its technology performance is through the purchase and importing of key technology from abroad and by collaborating with foreign companies. For example, it has obtained ESP technology through a license from Alstom in the 1980s and later in 2004 also obtained a license for fabric filter technology for particulate removal of coal-fired power plants. More

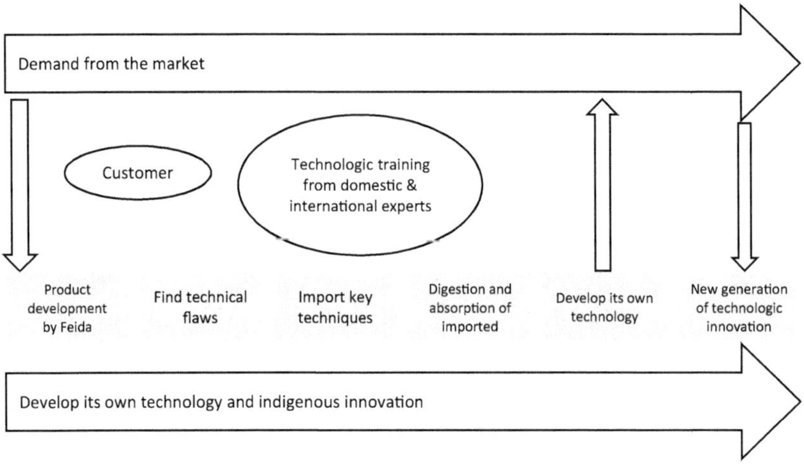

Fig. 4.3 Technologic innovation strategy in Feida

recently in 2013, it obtained wet ESP technology from Mitsubishi-Hitachi (MH) while in 2014 it established a joint venture with MH for environmental systems business development, where technology from MH would be customized for the domestic Chinese market by Feida and MH together in the joint venture.

Another pathway of improving technology performance is through research projects with local research institutions and universities. While collaborating with foreign companies or collaborating with research institutions might provide the core technology, further localized research will allow the company to make the technology suitable for the specific demands of the Chinese market. For instance, Chinese coal commonly has a higher proportion of sulphur compared to other countries, which creates technologic difficulty in desulfurization. The further improvement stage is called "secondary innovation". The products are promoted to local clients and the technology is protected through applying for domestic patents.

Feida's innovation strategy fits well with broader government policy. In order to encourage domestic companies to develop key innovative equipment, the National Development and Reform Commission (NDRC) launched a series of policies to support the development of "First Piece (Set) of Crucial High-Tech Equipment" (hereinafter referred to as the "first

Table 4.2 First product innovation on national and provincial level at Feida

Year	*Product*	*Certification*
2007	Electric precipitator for ultra-supercritical coal-fired plant with the power of 1000 MW	First product on the national level
2009	High efficiency bag-type dust collector for coal-fired units, with the power of 300 MW	First product on the provincial level
2011	Rotary electrode type electric precipitator for big coal-fired plants	First product on the national level
2012	PM2.5 pre-charged particle collecting device for coal-fired plant	First product on the provincial level
2014	PM2.5-controlling west electric precipitator	First product on the national level
2015	Low temperature electric precipitator	First product on the provincial level
2018	Phase change condensing dedusting and waste heat recovery and utilization integrated device	First product on the provincial level

equipment"), which is defined as "the crucial equipment of the country and relevant to comprehensive national strength and national security" (NDRC 2018). Feida owns a distinguished record in developing "first equipment". For instance, in the 1980s, Feida single handedly designed and built the very first power station ESP, with the capability of 50 MW (Wu et al. 2001). It was also the first enterprise to develop ESPs for circulating fluidized-bed boilers and alkali-recovered boilers in China. Feida has been awarded 7 different certifications as the developer of first equipment on national and provincial levels. The details of first product innovation is depicted in Table 4.2.

Factors Contributing to Technology Innovation

The technology innovation process in Feida is fostered both from the production and the user side. In Fig. 4.4, the blocks filled in black (technologic knowledge, labor/human resource, public authorities) represent the factors that most strongly affect innovation at Feida; the blocks filled in dark grey (transfer of knowledge, scientific knowledge) represent the second most influential factors; the blocks with light grey (capital, consumer markets) represent the third most important factors, and the groups represented in white (tools, societal groups, media) have the least influence on Feida's innovation.

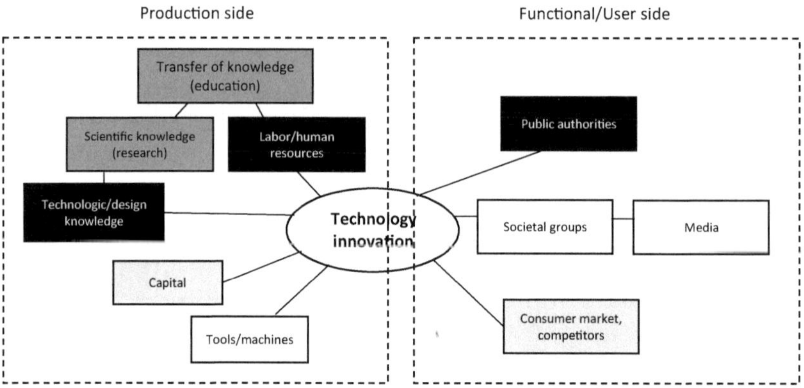

Fig. 4.4 How the innovation system affects innovation in Feida

Technologic/Design Knowledge, Labor/Human Resources, Public Authorities

Feida invests significantly in R&D, in terms of time and resources, reflecting the value that Feida sees in research and development as key for its innovation. Feida's manufacturing base covers a land area of 1600 acres with the State-level Enterprises Technical Center, National Postdoctoral Workstation, Engineering Design Academy, and five research institutes (ESP Research Institute, Pneumatic Conveying Research Institute, Desulfurization Research Institute, Fabric Filter Research Institute, Electric Control Research Institute), and further includes a large R&D team, research laboratory measurement facility, and a strong marketing network. As Feida realizes the significance of research, it makes large investments in R&D. Table 4.3 indicates the detailed information of R&D investment and R&D employees in 2016 and 2017. The figure of R&D investment and employees is around 114 million RMB in 2017 and 649 respectively (Feida 2017).

In addition, it holds more than 200 domestic patents in total, the majority being utility model patents but among them also 25 invention patents which are regarded as the most significant patents in the Chinese patent system. Figure 4.5 presents the patent applications from 2014 to 2017 by Feida. The motivation for patenting for utility model patents tends to be more protective, while invention patents are more important for developing new products and markets. The main function of protective patenting is to prevent potential imitation and allow legal ways for punishing violators;

Table 4.3 R&D investment and R&D employees in Feida

	2017	*2016*
R&D investment (million RMB)	114.19	110.72
The percentage of R&D investment over operating profit (%)	3	3
Number of R&D employees	649	627
The percentage of R&D employees over all staff (%)	16.58	14.71

whereas it is less focused on generating product innovation. The protective patenting behavior is triggered by the patent laws, giving rise to the increased patent value and knowledge, while strategic patenting through invention patents is more likely to respond to market needs and change. Feida's patents are all domestic Chinese patents, reflecting its current dominant focus on the domestic market. It also has not obtained international patents due to unfamiliarity with the international patent system. The company however is aiming to increase its income from international activities significantly so may have to consider developing an international patenting strategy.

For R&D, the quality of human resources, especially scientists and engineers, is one of the major factors that affect technologic innovation capacity. Therefore, Feida takes a lot of effort to establish a high-efficiency research team. The number of R&D staff in Feida has reached 649, accounting for 16.58% of all employees (Feida 2017). Among the R&D employees, 3 are state council experts with a special allowance and 72 are senior engineers. There are two divisions of R&D staff: design division and product development division. According to the interview, 20% of R&D technicians are working specifically on new products and innovation, and their performance will be evaluated based on the patent applications and new product development. For the design division staff, they work on specific commercial projects, from the beginning of contract negotiation, to field trips, testing, and after-service. Moreover, it provides incentives for staff to be involved in R&D, for staff in technical and marketing positions, and at a management level. It encourages employees to apply for patents. For instance, 50,000 RMB will be awarded for an invention patent and an "Innovation Award" is provided for technical and managerial innovation.

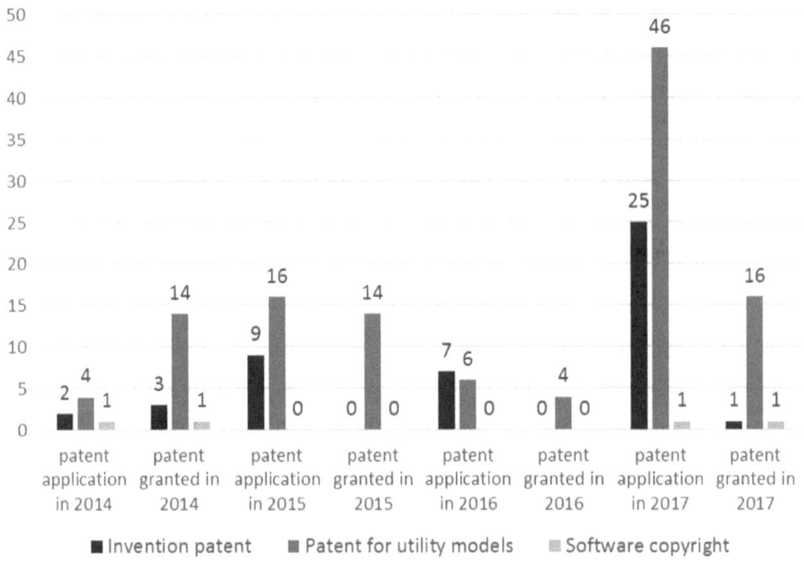

Fig. 4.5 Patent applications from 2014 to 2017 by Feida

Public Authorities

The public authorities refer to those entities who make new policies and regulations, including local government, international organizations such as the World Trade Organization (WTO), and central-level government bodies. The coal industry in China is mainly government-led and the monitoring system is still an administrative one, thus pressures for innovation for Feida to a large extent come from government standards and policies and are less market-driven. The main means of government intervention are through top-down mandates and through performance indices, such as measuring innovation on the number of patents that a company has. Being a state-owned enterprise, Feida is more responsive to government policies and regulations, compared to being driven by the (international) market or other entities.

Research Collaboration and Knowledge Transfer

Feida has collaborated with multiple research institutions and universities in various key research projects. Feida is involved in two State High-Tech

Development Programs, called the 863 program, in which it is the key investigator for specific sub-themes. The total funding of these two projects is more than 10 million RMB and Zhejiang University is a key collaborator for both projects. Feida also collaborates in research projects with other universities, e.g. the University of Nottingham Ningbo China, Northeastern University, Shandong University, and with state-owned companies involved in power generation in China, e.g. the China Huadian Corporation and the China Guodian Corporation. The cooperation with Zhejiang University focused on the detailed analysis of discharge patterns of PM 2.5 particles in power plants, as tiny particles emissions are different depending on the combustion process, and Feida is testing technology to further remove PM 2.5 particles from the exhaust gases of power plants. Related to this project, Feida, together with Shenhua Guohua Electric institute, also established a platform for the research on exhaust gas pollutants.

Feida does not only acquire technologic knowledge from collaborators through research projects, but also aims to improve its management and R&D capacity by collaborating with external institutions. For instance, the joint education of school and enterprise is adopted to cultivate talents. This practice can share common resources and advantages between each other and provide new opportunities for employee training. In 2011, a contract of expert training workstation was signed. Over 30 employees graduated with an Executive Master of Business Administration (EMBA) at Zhejiang University in 2017 (Zhejiang Academic and Expert Workstation 2017). In addition, Feida established a college for employee training in 2006, providing distance network education and face-to-face training. In 2017, it organized general technical and professional skill training on 140 occasions (Feida 2017).

Partnership and Market Competitors

Feida has developed partnerships (i.e. focusing on technology import and joint ventures) with international leading companies to improve its products. Table 4.4 presents examples of partnerships. For instance, a license agreement between ALSTOM and Feida had been made in 2004 in terms of fabric filter technology. It grants Feida rights to market, sell, and supply ALSTOM's proprietary fabric filter technology for particulate removal for the power generation industry in China. A joint venture company was set up in 2014 between Feida and Mitsubishi Hitachi Power Systems, Ltd. The new company is dedicated to providing comprehensive solutions for removal of PM 2.5 and other pollutants emitted by coal-fired power plants.

Table 4.4 Technologies imported from different countries by Feida

Year	*Company*	*Event*
1993	Dynamic Air	Import technology of pneumatic conveyance
1999	ABB	Import technology of NID semi-dry flue gas desulfurization
2004	ALSTOM	Import technology of bag-type dust remover
2013	Mitsubishi	Import technology of wet electro-static precipitator
2014	Mitsubishi	Joint venture between Feida and Mitsubishi

The management system of the environmental-protection industry in China is mainly directed and managed by the macro-policy (government policies, targets, and investments) and associations. This means companies in this industry are highly responsive to the regulation and policies, with less exposure to the market competition. In recent years, the coal power industry has gradually matured, and exhaust emission standards have become stricter and more strictly supervised. Government policy is also more focused on increasing other cleaner sources of energy, such as wind, solar, hydropower, and gas. This implies that the market for emission control of coal-fired power plants is not likely to expand and the demand will be smaller. One of the significant strategies for Feida is to expand internationally to explore new sources for business and profits. The international market for emission control systems of power plants is highly competitive. The main competitors include Alstom (before 2015, later became GE-Alstom), Babcock & Wilcox, Babcock, Hitachi, BPI, Doosan, and BHEL in India. Feida has been successful in some international projects; however, due to having limited experience in the international market and its limited exposure to international competition, Feida has also suffered some setbacks in its international expansion.

Societal Groups, Tools/Machines, and Media

The societal group refers to civil society organizations and non-governmental organizations (examples are Greenpeace or consumer groups), while the tools/machines category is about suppliers of materials, components, and tools (Geels 2004). These dynamic systems provide opportunities for companies to improve their products and achieve product innovation. Nevertheless, because of the nature of the industry and the relatively weak position of NGOs in China, Feida has paid less attention and effort to these groups.

Picture 4.3 Feida's electrostatic precipitator is visible here at the 370 MW Santa Maria Power Plant in Chile, operated by the Colbun group

Internationalization of Feida

International expansion is a vital strategy for Feida to expand its markets and to create new sources of income and profits. In recent years the company has set up subsidiaries in India and Singapore. In May 2016, with 70% of the shares owned by Feida, Feida International Power Technology Co. Ltd was established in Singapore. Its main business is in power generation based on biomass, waste, and coal and targeted toward Southeast Asia. Compared to Western competitors, Feida offers cost-effective products to the market, at about one-third of the price of Western companies. It has already generated some success in providing high-quality products to customers at affordable prices (see Picture 4.3 for example), and combining this with reliable after-sale service, which has earned the trust of various international customers.

Feida is utilizing two types of exporting strategy: the whole set exporting and direct exporting. Whole set exporting refers to its emission control systems being sold as part of a larger deal such as power plant construction through cooperation with big state-owned companies, including Dongfang Electric Corporation and TBEA Xi'an Electric Technology (Zhou

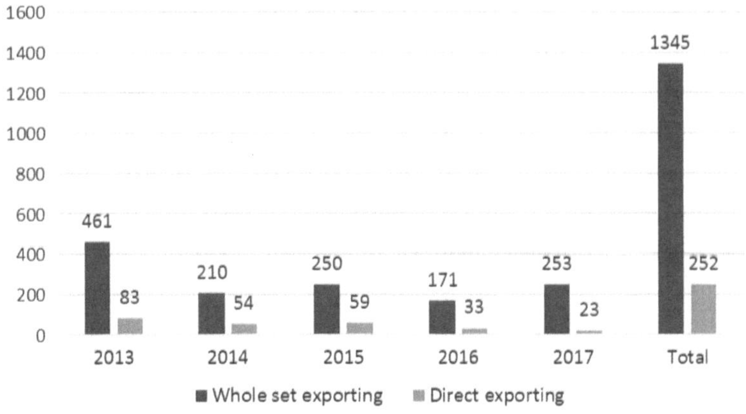

Fig. 4.6 Exporting data from 2013 to 2017

et al. 2015). Direct exporting refers to selling its emission control systems directly to international competitors. For whole-set exporting, the profits that Feida can make are limited, whereas this profit potential is higher in direct exporting. However, whole-set exporting involves limited political and management risk for Feida as these are covered by the main company in the transaction. The exporting data from 2013 to 2017 is depicted in Fig. 4.6.

It can be concluded from the data that the exporting trade is dominated by whole set exporting as it occupies 82%. For direct exporting Feida needs to strengthen its expertise in overseas markets to make sure that it will not suffer losses due to its inexperience with overseas local markets and politics. The problems Feida recently encountered in India with one of its projects showcase the importance of understanding overseas markets and having good relations with overseas partners and customers. Another important strategy for "going out" are projects signed with "One Belt One Road" countries. In 2017, Feida has been involved in a 2.2 billion dollars project in Jordan (Feida 2018).

An Example of a Leading Global Competitor, Alstom

With over 100 years experience, Alstom is experienced in power generation services, turnkey power plants, air quality control systems, and carbon capture equipment. With the Thermal Power sector sales figures of 6163 million euros in 2014, Alstom is a market leader in environmental-protection activities for the power generation sector. As Alstom's energy and power systems activities were acquired by the General Electric Company in 2015, we will mainly focus on the performance of its emission control systems for power generation before 2015.

The key priorities for the Alstom Thermal Power sector are to deliver operational excellence and good service to achieve high customer satisfaction. The company is involved in different development projects to improve the emission efficiency of coal-fired power plants, and these projects are partly funded by the European Union and the US Department of Energy. Alstom's innovation has been strongly R&D driven through intensive R&D programs over the past years. This R&D and innovation are guided by technologic and economic challenges of reducing emissions of fossil fuel-based electricity production. There are 17 "R&D execution" centers across Europe, North America, and Asia (Alstom 2011). Their major responsibility ranges from technical support, to conducting cutting-edge activities that will create innovative products. It is estimated that the total number of Thermal Power R&D employees and its associated partners is over 2500, among which 10 are Senior Experts, 132 are Experts, and 430 are Principal engineers (Alstom 2014). Alstom applied for several hundred international patents worldwide in 2013, half of which involved innovative mechanical design, chemical process, and new or improved cycles. With the strategic focus on advanced combustion, steam cycle, and steam turbine blade technologies, Alstom aims to achieve a 50% reduction of emissions from fossil-based power plants.

Specific development programs are built to encourage employee contribution and ensure the company is at the edge of the most sophisticated techniques. The Expert Program is valued by Alstom to form a specific innovation community. Additionally, in 2008, Alstom launched the "Alstom Innovation Awards", which were designed to reward employees for the development and implementation of innovative solutions. In 2011, over 1100 employees from 22 countries were involved in this competition, with 399 applications received that year (Alstom 2011).

Alstom implements a series of management procedures and tools to train qualified personnel, stimulate the innovative mind, and encourage the expression and the sharing of ideas and knowledge. In July 2013, a "Learning Solutions and Alstom University" was set up for face-to-face and distance training and learning. The number of trainees at Alstom University in 2014 was 28,766 (Alstom 2014).

Furthermore, Alstom keeps good relationships with academic and scientific partners across the world, to access facilities, expertise, and research talent and accelerate the time-to-market product innovation. They have established more than 350 partnerships with universities, and Alstom actively participates in all important associations and standard-setting bodies.

Challenges for Feida

With its goal of international expansion, one of the challenges that Feida faces is its limited experience with and knowledge of overseas markets. The main business of Feida is located domestically in the environmental-protection equipment for coal-fired plants. The viable domestic market tends to be shrinking and is highly competitive, as there is excess capacity in thermal power generation while renewable technology development is supported by the local government. Therefore, international expansion is essential for Feida. As India has a strong base in coal-fired power plants, and is facing challenges to limit the air emission of these power plants, it comes as a priority for Feida's internationalization under the strategy of "going out". However, the company has encountered problems in the Indian market as it had difficulty adapting to this different international environment, and has a lack of management experience, talent, expertise, and knowledge of international markets. Consequently, it suffered a significant loss in 2017 on a collaborative project in India with BGR Energy Systems Limited.

Part of the challenge Feida is facing is due to its limited exposure to the market, international environment, and competition. With the efforts and contribution in four decades, Feida has obtained a leading position in the air quality industry in the domestic market. The nature of its industry in China requires the company to put significant effort into building good relationships with (local) government(s) and responding to their needs. This has implied that the company has been much less exposed to the international market and the competitive pressures from international markets. It has also led to a technologic development trajectory that is mostly domestic and only involves very limited international activities, projects, and R&D efforts. This is reflected in the gap between Feida and international leading companies such as Alstom, with regard to patenting behaviors, international R&D projects, and training and talents programs.

Ways to Move Forward for Feida

Some of the ways forward for Feida include further development of its international innovation activities, a strengthening of its R&D and innovation activities with international and external partners, and finally strengthening of its talent training and recruitment.

The first suggestion is to implement more internal innovation actions and programs. A series of management procedures and tools (e.g. incubators, ventures) are encouraged to build an innovative and dynamic atmosphere, stimulate the innovative mind, and encourage the expression and the sharing of ideas and knowledge. For instance, SUEZ, a leading company in the environmental-protection domain, established an experimentation lab within its company, while Siemens developed open innovation activities to enhance innovation projects and activities among its employees, cross-cutting various departments. Acting as an incubator, it helps to share the innovative minds, and nurture and support projects in terms of commercial and industrial support.

It is also recommended that Feida can increase its R&D and innovation activities with external and especially international partners. Competition in a more open environment can help companies to quickly respond to market changes and customer needs. Feida can also promote "open innovation", where cooperation with academic and scientific partners is encouraged. Moreover, partnership culture is encouraged to be active through local public or private players (industrial, financial, or non-profit org) with an in-depth knowledge of the local context. This could substantially decrease the potential cost, share the technology and information, and help Feida to develop dynamic and innovative products. Programs such as an incubator with top universities, and venture programs for SMEs and innovative companies, could be good examples to support innovation eco-systems.

The final suggestion is associated with developing systematic employee training and recruiting more talents. Various training programs and continuing training initiatives framework are advised to help employees to learn specific knowledge or skills in the industry. This includes domestic and international training of personnel by top industry experts, opportunities of attending relevant conferences, and the high-value-added courses with academic professionals. In addition, more talents who have access to international business knowledge and cutting-edge technology, and are aware of differences in foreign institutional environments, need to be recruited.

Further Investigation

1. Examine how Feida has been able to develop a strong brand both domestically and internationally. Is there a significant difference between the strength of its domestic brand and international brand? Discuss some of the factors that explain this difference.
2. Why may R&D and innovation be important in brand building? To what extent has it been important for Feida? What are the major approaches that Feida has used for innovation and brand building and how is this different from an international competitor such as Alstom? What key recommendation would you give to Feida to further strengthen its innovation and branding strategy?
3. Feida has a strong presence in the emission control systems for power plants and is now considering to further develop other areas of business including solid waste treatment and water pollution treatment. Discuss what the rationale is for Feida to consider moving into these areas and assess current strengths and weaknesses of Feida that could help or inhibit them to be successful in these new business areas.

References

Agarwal, Sanjeev, M. Krishna Erramilli, and Chekitan S. Dev. "Market orientation and performance in service firms: Role of innovation." *Journal of Services Marketing* 17, no. 1 (2003): 68–82.

Alstom. "Annual Report of Alstom for 2011," 2011, accessed July 5, 2018. http://www.alstom.com/Global/Group/Resources/Documents/Investors%20document/DDR%202011-12%20VA%20FINAL.pdf.

Alstom. "Annual Report of Alstom for 2014," 2014, accessed July 15, 2018. http://www.alstom.com/Global/Group/Resources/Documents/Investors%20document/ALSTOM%20DDR-2014-15_UK_MEL.PDF.

Beverland, Michael B., Julie Napoli, and Francis Farrelly. "Can all brands innovate in the same way? A typology of brand position and innovation effort." *Journal of Product Innovation Management* 27, no. 1 (2010): 33–48.

Feida. "Feida 2017 Corporate Social Responsibility Report," 2017, accessed July 22, 2018. http://quotes.money.163.com/f10/ggmx_600526_4273542.html.

Feida. "Entering Middle East Market Under the 'Belt and Road' Strategy," 2018, accessed July 13, 2018. https://www.feidaep.com/ZXDT/show/id/251.html.

Geels, Frank W. "From sectoral systems of innovation to socio-technical systems: Insights about dynamics and change from sociology and institutional theory." *Research Policy* 33, nos. 6–7 (2004): 897–920.

Hofman, Peter S. *Innovation and institutional change: The transition to a sustainable electricity system*. Enschede: University of Twente/CSTM, 2005.

Hofman, Peter S., and Theo de Bruijn. "The emergence of sustainable innovations: Key factors and regional support structures." In *Facilitating sustainable innovation through collaboration*, 115–133. Dordrecht: Springer, 2010.

Kapferer, Jean-Noël. *The new strategic brand management: Advanced insights and strategic thinking*. London: Kogan Page Publishers, 2012.

Lin, Boqiang. *China energy outlook 2017*. Beijing: Peking University Press, 2017.

Metz, Bert, Ogunlade Davidson, Rob Swart, and Jiahua Pan, eds. *Climate change 2001: Mitigation—Contribution of working group III to the third assessment report of the Intergovernmental Panel on Climate Change*. Vol. 3. Cambridge: Cambridge University Press, 2001.

NDRC. "Promoting Demonstrative Application of the First Piece (Set) of Major Technological Equipment, Opinions of NDRC, MOST, MIIT, et al. Document number 558 of the National Development and Reform Commission," 2018, accessed October 16, 2018. http://lawinfochina.com/display.aspx?id=28143&lib=law&SearchKeyword=&SearchCKeyword.

NEA. "13th Five-Year Plan for Power Development," 2016, accessed October 18, 2018. https://www.sohu.com/a/122347707_464105.

Srinivasan, Shuba, Koen Pauwels, Jorge Silva-Risso, and Dominique M. Hanssens. "Product innovations, advertising, and stock returns." *Journal of Marketing* 73, no. 1 (2009): 24–43.

Weerawardena, Jay, Aron O'Cass, and Craig Julian. "Does industry matter? Examining the role of industry structure and organizational learning in innovation and brand performance." *Journal of Business Research* 59, no. 1 (2006): 37–45.

Wu, Hua, Xiaobo Wu, and Ying Sun. "The technological innovation strategy at Feida (菲达集团的可升级技术创新战略 in Chinese)." *Economic Management Journal* 1 (2001): 48–50.

Yuan, Jiahai, Chunning Na, Qi Lei, Minpeng Xiong, Jingsheng Guo, and Zheng Hu. "Coal use for power generation in China." *Resources, Conservation and Recycling* 129 (2018): 443–453.

Zhejiang Academic and Expert Workstation. "The Establishment of an Academic and Expert Workstation in Feida," 2017, accessed July 9, 2018. http://yszx.zast.org.cn/html/yszjgzz/gb2312/.

Zhou, Zhiming, Keyuan Ma, and Weng Junfei. "One Belt and One Road, Cultivation of Key Technology." *Zhejiang Daily*, December 14, 2015, 1.

CHAPTER 5

Customer Orientation and Brand Performance: A Study of ROBAM

Zi Wang, Yue Huang, Jun Luo and Xuan Feng

Introduction

After the global financial crisis in 2008, traditional production capacity could no longer meet the increasing needs of consumers' daily lives. A booming industrial transformation involving the areas of information technology, biotechnology, new energy, and new materials has promoted profound changes in manufacturing models and industry patterns. Aiming at optimizing the structure of the domestic industry, the proposal of 'China Made 2025', which states China's will to move up the value chain and reinvent itself from a world manufacturing production workshop into a world-class industrialized power, has undoubtedly started a new chapter for Chinese manufacturing enterprise. As a company/brand with the highest market share and the largest production scale of domestic high-end kitchen appliances within the industry, ROBAM (Picture 5.1) was selected to be one of the first batch of brands certified with 'China made'. The key determinant of ROBAM's great success is recognized to be its customer-

Z. Wang (✉) · Y. Huang · J. Luo · X. Feng
University of Nottingham Ningbo China, Ningbo, China
e-mail: bixzw2@nottingham.edu.cn

M. J. Liu and J. Luo (eds.), *China Branding*,
https://doi.org/10.1007/978-981-13-9318-1_5

Picture 5.1 The manufacturing base of ROBAM

oriented position by seeing through consumers' demands and penetrating into their daily lifestyle.

Customer Orientation

Customer orientation (CO) is defined as the belief that puts the customer's interest first, while not excluding those of all other stakeholders for the purpose of developing a long-term viable business (e.g., Brady and Cronin 2001; Slater and Narver 1994; Deshpandé et al. 1993; Webster 1988). Customer orientation requires firms to consider customer satisfaction as essential at the core of every decision in order to achieve superior business success (cf. Caruana et al. 1997; Jaworski and Kohli 1993).

A few studies claim that customer-oriented brands create products which transform market needs (e.g., Jaworski and Kohli 1993; Narver and Slater 1990). Narver and Slater (1990) also indicate that customer-oriented behavior leads to superior innovation and greater new product success. In practice, even though the innovation is made by inner development efforts, and aims to act upon the market, the innovative culture assumes that successful innovation acquires sufficient understanding of the market's underlying response (O'Cass and Ngo 2007). Based on the external orientation, innovativeness could help companies to recognize the significance of the brand, as both the commercialization of the innovations and a valuable tool to get closer to customers' needs, since the brand lends credibility and security (Aaker 2007).

Brady and Cronin (2001) also argue that customer-oriented firms outperform competitors by anticipating the developing needs of consumers and responding with goods and services to which superior value and greater satisfaction are consistently attributed. In addition, to provide superior value to the external customer, it is essential that superior value is offered at each stage of the value chain, that is to say, internal suppliers need to concentrate on satisfying the requirements of their internal customers, demonstrating an internal customer orientation, which could ensure the effective delivery of a customer and market orientation throughout the organization (Hauser et al. 1996). It is also recognized in marketing literature that all employees of a firm are internal customers (Gummesson 1987; George 1990; Lukas and Maignan 1996). The concept of an internal customer indicates that each employee is both a supplier and a customer to the others within the firm (Grönroos 1981; Foreman and Money 1995) so that internal customers can generate goods and services for the end customers (Mohrw-Jackson 1991). Besides, the significance of developing an internal customer orientation has also been emphasized in the service literature. Berry (1981) acknowledged the importance of the internal employees in dealing with the external customer, identifying that employees' satisfaction and support of a firm's overall marketing strategy was vital for external customer satisfaction.

ROBAM—The Rise of China Brands

As one of the most well-known and popular professional kitchen appliance brands in China, ROBAM has always attached great importance to customer-oriented innovation and brand building. Positioned as the leader of Chinese high-end kitchen brands, ROBAM has won many honors over 40 years such as the 'China Quality Silver Award', 'China Top Brand', 'China's 500 most valuable brands' and was also one of the first batch brands

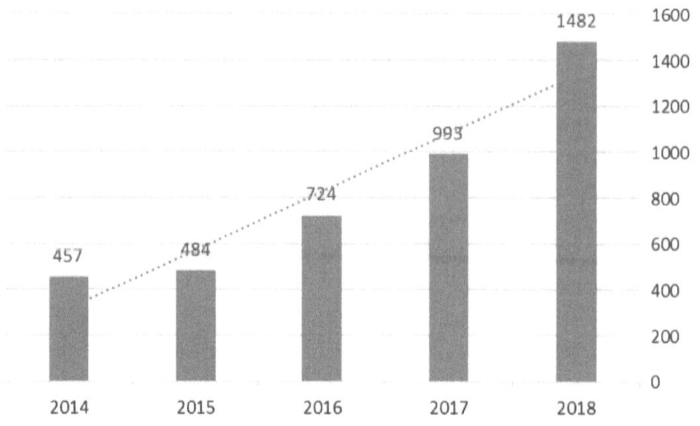

Fig. 5.1 ROBAM's operating revenue

certified by 'ZhejiangMade'. Through years of effort, ROBAM has founded the first domestic innovation industrial park of kitchen appliances and the first smart factory within the industry. As a domestic leading brand of high-end kitchen appliances, the sales volume of ROBAM has come first in the global market since 2015. Since its listing in 2010, the compound growth rate of ROBAM's operating revenue has achieved 30% for the following six years, of which the net profit growth rate has reached over 40% (Fig. 5.1). In 2015, representing China's high-end manufacturing, ROBAM participated in the Milan Expo, which promoted the brand image and enhanced its global influence. In March 2018, ROBAM built up the first intelligent manufacturing T-Park that could produce 2.5 million kitchen appliances a year, which is the benchmark for the upgrade of 'China Intelligent Made'. One of the key factors which has led to ROBAM's success is considered to be its customer-oriented operation principle. Considering the new circumstances of the global economic slowdown and fast technology upgrading within the kitchen industry, ROBAM has implemented initiative strategies which include enhancing technology and institutional innovation and promoting cultural confidence, based on the customer-oriented business philosophy. The following chapters will illustrate the above three perspectives.

Technology Innovation

Products

The effectiveness of originating and implementing customer-oriented technical innovations has always been viewed as a key developing tactic and brand asset for the ROBAM company. Aiming at developing high-end kitchen appliances and providing better integral solutions for customers' kitchen life, ROBAM has been putting constant efforts into their product innovation. For example, ROBAM has obtained a number of patent certifications over the years such as the 'A++' free wash hood, main fire-centered gas stoves, the 'UP' electric pressure pot, etc. With the acceleration of consumption upgrading in China, the categories of new emerging products have grown rapidly with huge market potential. As the first overseas research and development platform of the Chinese kitchen industry, ROBAM's California Innovation Centre (RCIC) launched in Silicon Valley in 2017 (Wu 2017). Focusing on the research and innovation of IoT and artificial intelligence, it marks the beginning of ROBAM's digital intelligent manufacturing integration with worldwide advanced technology, which is the first step of ROBAM's entry into the global market and a significant move for its customer-oriented business development.

CCS Central Fume Purification System

It has always been ROBAM's guideline to focus on the enhancement of customer satisfaction and the resolution of users' pain points. ROBAM's previous investigation showed that there generally existed obstructed smoke evacuation in the public chimneys of residential areas, which especially affected the residents who lived on the ground floor. Considering this, the technical team of ROBAM has developed a new CCS central fume purification system which, to a great extent, solves the soot blockage problems in rush hours. To be specific, instead of the traditional electric motor, ROBAM installs a new mainframe on the top of the public flue of each residential building which provides strong smoke extraction by intelligent power distribution. Through this technology innovation, the exhaust efficiency of the ground-floor residence has improved over 40% and the purifying rate of smoke has reached 99.5%, which has made pronounced contributions to the urban air purification. It is also worth mentioning that the pioneering CCS central fume purification system has gained eight significant patent certifications domestically. In parallel, an automatic boost mode has also been added on ROBAM's extractor hoods in order to prevent the harm of lampblack flowing backward, which is a successful example of ROBAM's customer-centric practice.

Green Revolution
For the vital interests of the customers, ROBAM has proposed a circular economy developing strategy targeted at creating a green ecological system for citizens' lives, which is also known as 'ROBAM's Green Revolution'. The release of ROBAM's double suction hood of the fourth generation in 2017 has reinforced its initiative environmental developing strategy within the industry. Although large suction has drawn the attention of many companies, only a few of them have addressed the kitchen noise while improving the efficiency of the extractor hood. For the purpose of enhancing consumers' kitchen experience, the research team of ROBAM has adopted an external rotor electric machine to readjust the hood structure, which reduces the unnecessary noise to a great extent while achieving 30% of energy conservation. In addition, in order to meet customers' health consumption requirements, the agricultural waste purification tank D102 is designed to help ensure food security for customers by removing the potential pesticide residues and pathogenic bacterium, of which the removal efficiency could reach 99%.

O2O Kitchen Resource Infospace
In order to always put customers first, it is important to gain a better insight into consumers' spending habits and their psychological anticipation before any business activities (Flint et al. 2011). ROBAM has launched a new 'O2O Kitchen Resource Infospace' development project (Ren and Jiang 2016) aimed at bringing consumers a fresh eco-kitchen experience, which was the first example of the domestic kitchen exploration hall. In order to stimulate effective demand, O2O Kitchen Resource Infospace allows customers to experience all the categories of ROBAM's kitchen resources including kitchen appliances, kitchen furniture, cooking utensils, cooking ingredients, and even free cooking classes. Apart from introducing product parameters, the sales assistants pay much attention to sharing the ideas of life aesthetics with customers and encouraging individuals to return to their families. Additionally, all of the resource information in the infospace is connected to both the server platform and the suppliers, which provides consumers with an entire service process from experiencing to purchasing while realizing real-time order management. Moreover, apart from a one-stop shopping experience, O2O Kitchen Source Infospace also

gives consumers a communication platform to share cooking and healthy lifestyle ideas, which has increased the potential brand equity imperceptibly. Thereby, ROBAM's innovation of the kitchen infospace has explored a new path for the traditional industries that have been strongly impacted by online sales and provided an effective solution for the current decline in sales efficiency of offline stores.

Intelligent Warehouse Management System (IWMS)
On one hand, the domestic market of smart home appliances has developed rapidly since 2014, which was an outcome of the development of internet technology and consumers' quality of living. On the other hand, the annual sales of ROBAM has increased from less than one million to around five million since its listing in 2010, which brings a large demand of higher logistic efficiency and bigger storage capacity. Therefore, ROBAM set up the biggest digital integrated manufacturing and logistics base in China in 2015 (Picture 5.2), which marked the realization of the automation, intellectualization, and informationization of ROBAM. Thereby, the establishment of the central control system has achieved centralized product management through computer scheduling and monitoring, which substantively improves the productivity. The robotic system makes palletizing tasks more accurate and eliminates the burden on the workforce. Moreover, the self-developed circular shuttle has substantially saved storage space while improving conveying efficiency. As a result, ROBAM's annual output of kitchen electrical products can reach two million, seven hundred thousand while holding the capacity of eight million machines working simultaneously. Notably, apart from greatly expanding the storage capacity and improving the logistic efficiency, IWMS of ROBAM also makes it possible to process consumers' personalized orders on time and satisfy customers' diverse demand to a large extent due to ROBAM's automated high-rise warehouse and auto-sorting. In addition, aimed at enhancing consumption experience, ROBAM's official app also enables customers to track the logistic information of their orders, which is another potent embodiment of ROBAM's customer-oriented operation philosophy.

ROKI System
The launch of the new intelligent system-ROKI of ROBAM has not only been a milestone in the domestic kitchen appliance industry, but also a significant attempt of ROBAM's customer-oriented business development. Different from ROBAM's conventional extractor hood, ROKI makes it

Picture 5.2 Intelligent manufacturing system and intelligent warehouse management system

viable for consumers to trace the whole product value chain through its app. In terms of the use phase, ROKI could intelligently control the heat and cooking time as well as provide varieties of recipes, which is especially useful to those young citizens who cannot cook. Moreover, by synchronizing with ROBAM's mobile app, customers are able to receive reminders from ROKI to turn off the heat in time, which could help reduce kitchen security risks to a certain degree. According to Zhao (2017), the CTO of ROBAM, the fusion of extractor hoods and wearable devices such as smart watches, smart wristbands, etc., will be their new developing focus. In addition, the intelligent procurement and distribution system also seems to draw much attention to ROBAM's innovation team. Undoubtedly, the implementation of customer-oriented intellectualization has become an irresistible growing trend for domestic industries, which is in accordance with the prospect of 'intelligently China Made' and Chinese ecological transformation.

Institutional Innovation

New-Type Partnership—A Shared Allocation Mechanism

As Boluhongxing hardware factory, the predecessor of ROBAM, used to be a product of Chinese planned economy back in 1979, the collective spirit of sharing benefits and risks has always been part of ROBAM's corporate culture, which is the very beginning of ROBAM's customer-oriented operation principle. The control agent system implemented by ROBAM's sales territory decentralizes operational rights, financial power, and personnel power to agencies, which builds up a close partnership between ROBAM and its distributors. In 2013, ROBAM decided to launch their 'Thousand Partners' program that encouraged core employees to participate in ROBAM's business through dividends or shareholdings, and subsequently transform into its business partners. For those who have the will and ability to lead the development of the regional market, ROBAM will set up a platform to provide technologic and financial support. However, all the potential candidates must be chosen from internal employees with over three years' working experience to ensure their loyalty. As for the agent branches, ROBAM transformed them from self-operation to joint-stock operation in order to achieve the binding of interests between the agent company and the parent firm. Hence, all the first-level agents need to be the key employees sent from the headquarters and the establishment funds are supposed to be composed of their credit line and self-raised capital. Furthermore, in 2014, ROBAM developed a new-type partnership targeted at the managers of the new joint-stock agent companies and the top executives who were the shareholders of ROBAM's agent companies. This benefit-sharing mechanism awards both the employees and the channel partners surplus profits after achieving annual targets, which has mobilized the initiatives of the related staff with entrepreneurial spirit and has also greatly enhanced their career loyalty. Until 2018, the total amount of employees' shareholdings accounted for 0.42% of ROBAM's stock, which highly improves the satisfaction of ROBAM's internal customers and verifies ROBAM's customer orientation from another aspect. In parallel, the sharing mechanism of internal resources and values has also been applied in other sections such as the 'Super Factory Project' and 'Quality Crowdfunding Project', which also stimulated ROBAM's developing potential and inspired the initiatives of employees.

SuperWorks—A Public Innovation Platform
As an innovative and entrepreneurial platform, SuperWorks of ROBAM provides technical support and services to capable entrepreneurial teams and individuals aiming at fully realizing its customer-oriented philosophy. This model doesn't only offer a lot of cutting-edge technology assistance, but also new ideas for technical research and the development of ROBAM. In addition, SuperWorks has encouraged internal and external innovations from the bottom-up, which is of great significance in many fields within the industry such as talent selection, technology reserve, and new business model exploration. For example, ROBAM's air purifying hood, the first project of SuperWorks, can highly improve the kitchen air quality while absorbing the oil fumes. It has brought together the core employees in each industrial chain to form this project group from the departments of technology, product design, service, logistics, and marketing, which means all the employees involved in the product life cycle are shareholders. This project successfully completed the 100,000 RMB crowdfunding target in JD.com Crowdfunding within 2 hours, and even doubled the crowdfunding target on the second day, which broke the record of JD.com Crowdfunding under the same product category. The platform of SuperWorks has inspired both ROBAM's internal and external customers to a great extent, which could be seen as more progress ROBAM has made in achieving customer orientation.

Picture 5.3 ROBAM's product poster

Cultural Confidence

Culture is defined as the 'collective programming of the mind which distinguishes the members of one group or category of people from those of another' and it refers more tangibly to relatively enduring personality characteristics that are 'common or standardized in a given society' (Inkeles and Levinson 1969). Culture is regarded as the most pervasive and thorny factor which influences consumer behavior. Individuals draw on consumer goods to express cultural groupings and principles, and to craft and carry on ideas and lifestyles (McCracken 1986). Successful marketing strategies involve synchronizing product attributes and promotional appeals with those consumer attitudes fashioned by individual and cultural values (Cleveland et al. 2013). Since ROBAM mainly focuses on the domestic market, it is essential to exert the cultural influence on Chinese consumers' behavior (Picture 5.3), which is in accordance with its customer-oriented principle.

Culture and Products

Chinese people are proud of the time-honored and profound Chinese diet culture, which is an essential part of Chinese traditional culture. In China, people's happiness and sadness, marriage, and social intercourse are all closely related to diet. In other words, diet to some extent is equal to life. Based on this cultural confidence, ROBAM has the customer-oriented mission of 'to make customers be happier in cooking, feel warm in the kitchen, and have a better life'. ROBAM aims to bring a new life to Chinese traditional cooking culture through technical development based on customers' demands. One example could be the kitchen ventilator. Chinese kitchens have their own particularity, as cooking emissions is one of the key problems caused by some Chinese traditional cooking methods. Excessive oil fumes from kitchens seriously affect residents' living quality and space. However, many kitchen ventilators with a foreign brand are unable to solve this problem due to their insufficient suction ability. As a result, Guocheng Yu, the chief engineer of the ROBAM kitchen ventilators, believes that a kitchen suitable for Chinese people should satisfy their needs while cooking. One significant need for them is to reduce the oil fumes caused by frying and many other cooking methods. Consequently, as a customer-oriented company, ROBAM kept on investing in the R&D of kitchen ventilators to solve this problem.

Moreover, as one of the Chinese traditional cooking methods, steaming makes food healthier than conventional cooking methods such as grilling, baking, or frying as steaming retains the vitamins and minerals. By combining modern technology with traditional Chinese cooking techniques, ROBAM launched the S228 steamer, which has the cooking model of 'fast steaming and slow stewing' as well as the function of drying the box, in order to meet Chinese customers' needs. This steamer can hold 3 layers of large steaming trays and is also able to steam a whole chicken or fish. Based on technologic innovation, combined with in-depth insights into Chinese traditional cooking culture and contemporary Chinese life, ROBAM wants to create a Chinese kitchen with a new style.

Culture and Content Marketing

As defined by the Content Market Institute, 'content marketing is the marketing and Business Process for creating and distributing relevant and valuable content to attract, acquire, and engage a clearly defined and understood target audience - with the objective of driving profitable customer action' (Content Marketing Institute 2018). A brand identity and voice could be shaped and created by the content, which might also make a company and its products relevant, believable, and accessible. Lieb (2012) believes that the internet and digital channels overwhelmingly account for the preponderance of content marketing outlets. For ROBAM, 70% of its target consumers are aged 25–35. In order to attract the attention of these consumers and fit their needs, ROBAM has to learn how to communicate with them by content marketing through the internet and the mobile internet. In 2016, ROBAM sponsored a network program 'Sister is hungry', a talk show about cooking and food. ROBAM chose this program because this show was recorded in the kitchen and ROBAM wanted to show the audience that they aim to create a Chinese kitchen with new style. Moreover, in the same year, ROBAM took advantage of the hot topic of the Rio Olympics by jointly recording an internet program with NetEase, named 'Champion's House'. In this internet program, a cozy 'Champion's house' was decorated in Rio and athletes who won gold medals in the Rio Olympics were invited to taste traditional Chinese food and interact with Chinese audiences in this house.

In addition, in order to create a new retail system covering physical stores, e-commerce, mobile terminals, and social media, so as to achieve a comprehensive integration of online and offline marketing, ROBAM made a plan regarding the contribution of 100 cultural experience halls with the theme of 'Kitchen Resource' to communicate with customers through a new experiential retail mode. In 2012, ROBAM built the first organic experience hall about kitchen culture in China, with the name 'Kitchen Resource'. This cultural experience hall integrates humanistic science and technology and the concept of low-carbon environmental protection with Liangzhu culture, which was the last Neolithic jade culture in the Yangtze River Delta of China. Liangzhu culture, as explained by ROBAM, had promoted the development of cooking utensils as well as the development of Chinese cooking and its culture through people's excellent skills in crafting black pottery from 3400 BC to 2250 BC.

ROBAM built the cultural experience hall, 'the source of kitchen', as a platform for the company to communicate with consumers and to share the healthy and relaxing culture about kitchen life with Chinese customers. ROBAM's cultural experience hall displays different kinds of products, including kitchen appliances, integrated cabinets, kitchen soft packaging, cooking utensils, ingredients, and cooking courses, which are all available for customers to experience. Through activities and the environment in the cultural experience hall, ROBAM wants to show their customers that the kitchen is no longer just a place for making, but also a space to enjoy cooking and communicate with family members and friends.

Summary

ROBAM has accomplished the transformation of the traditional kitchen industry in China and gained significant market return by adopting a series of customer-oriented business strategies covering the whole product life cycle. The success of ROBAM marks a great advancement of 'China Made' in the new situation of economic development on a global scale, which guides the future development of the domestic kitchen industry and gives worthy insights to manufacturing industries as to how to adapt to today's consumption upgrading and industrial conversion. It has also undoubtedly provided valuable reference for customer-based brand building and the establishment of brand differentiation. However, there exists some potential challenges in the business development of ROBAM. For example, the growth of ROBAM's annual net profit has shown a declining trend since 2010 under intensifying competition. Meanwhile, the integrated high-end home appliance giants such as Haier and Midea are trying to take a share of the spoils with their multidimensional advantages. In addition, the downturn of the domestic housing market and the price fluctuation of raw materials have also brought a negative influence on ROBAM's future development. Besides, how to make ROBAM go global under the policy of 'One Belt One Road' has become a new concern for the decision maker.

Further Investigation

1. What approaches does ROBAM need to apply to achieve customer orientation?
2. Why do you think customer orientation is of great importance to business performance?
3. What would you do to further enhance ROBAM's brand awareness if you were the brand manager?
4. What strategies do you think ROBAM should adopt in the next five to ten years?

References

Aaker, David. "Innovation: Brand it or lose it." *California Management Review* 50, no. 1 (2007): 8–24.

Berry, Leonard L. "The employee as customer." *Journal of Retail Banking* 3, no. 1 (1981): 33–40.

Brady, Michael K., and J. Joseph Cronin Jr. "Customer orientation: Effects on customer service perceptions and outcome behaviors." *Journal of Service Research* 3, no. 3 (2001): 241–251.

Caruana, Albert, B. Ramaseshan, and Michael T. Ewing. "Market orientation and organizational commitment in the Australian public sector." *International Journal of Public Sector Management* 10, no. 4 (1997): 294–303.

Cleveland, Mark, Michel Laroche, and Ranim Hallab. "Globalization, culture, religion, and values: Comparing consumption patterns of Lebanese Muslims and Christians." *Journal of Business Research* 66, no. 8 (2013): 958–967.

Content Marketing Institute. "What Is Content Marketing?" accessed July 16, 2018. http://contentmarketinginstitute.com/what-is-content-marketing/.

Deshpandé, Rohit, John U. Farley, and Frederick E. Webster Jr. "Corporate culture, customer orientation, and innovativeness in Japanese firms: A quadrad analysis." *Journal of Marketing* 57, no. 1 (1993): 23–37.

Flint, Daniel J., Christopher P. Blocker, and Philip J. Boutin Jr. "Customer value anticipation, customer satisfaction and loyalty: An empirical examination." *Industrial Marketing Management* 40, no. 2 (2011): 219–230.

Foreman, Susan K., and Arthur H. Money. "Internal marketing: Concepts, measurement and application." *Journal of Marketing Management* 11, no. 8 (1995): 755–768.

George, William R. "Internal marketing and organizational behavior: A partnership in developing customer-conscious employees at every level." *Journal of Business Research* 20, no. 1 (1990): 63–70.

Grönroos, Christian. "Internal marketing—An integral part of marketing theory." *Marketing of Services* 236 (1981): 238.

Gummesson, Evert. "Using internal marketing to develop a new culture—The case of ericsson quality." *Journal of Business & Industrial Marketing* 2, no. 3 (1987): 23–28.

Hauser, John R., Duncan I. Simester, and Birger Wernerfelt. "Internal customers and internal suppliers." *Journal of Marketing Research* 33, no. 3 (1996): 268–280.

Inkeles, Alex, and Daniel J. Levinson. "National character: The study of modal personality and sociocultural systems." *The Handbook of Social Psychology* 4 (1969): 418–506.

Jaworski, Bernard J., and Ajay K. Kohli. "Market orientation: Antecedents and consequences." *Journal of Marketing* 57, no. 3 (1993): 53–70.

Lieb, Rebecca. *Content marketing: Think like a publisher—How to use content to market online and in social media.* Que Publishing, 2012.

Lukas, Bryan A., and Isabelle Maignan. "Striving for quality: The key role of internal and external customers." *Journal of Market-Focused Management* 1, no. 2 (1996): 175–187.

McCracken, Grant. "Culture and consumption: A theoretical account of the structure and movement of the cultural meaning of consumer goods." *Journal of Consumer Research* 13, no. 1 (1986): 71–84.

Mohrw-Jackson, Iris. “Broadening the market orientation: An added focus on internal customers.” *Human Resource Management* 30, no. 4 (1991): 455–467.

Narver, John C., and Stanley F. Slater. “The effect of a market orientation on business profitability.” *Journal of Marketing* 54, no. 4 (1990): 20–35.

O’Cass, Aron, and Liem Viet Ngo. “Market orientation versus innovative culture: Two routes to superior brand performance.” *European Journal of Marketing* 41, no. 7/8 (2007): 868–887.

Ren, Fang., and Jiang, Hong. “ROBAM Electric builts an intelligent warehousing and logistics center. (老板电器打造智能仓储物流中心 in Chinese)” *Logistics and Material Handling* 11 (2016): 80–84.

Slater, Stanley F., and John C. Narver. “Market orientation, customer value, and superior performance.” *Business Horizons* 37, no. 2 (1994): 22–29.

Webster Jr, Frederick E. “The rediscovery of the marketing concept.” *Business Horizons* 31, no. 3 (1988): 29–39.

Wu, Zhijun. “ROBAM Electric sets up ‘Three Outlooks’, and Chinese kitchen electricity starts to go global. (老板电器树“三观”中国[U+53A8]电开启全球时间 in Chinese)” *China Brand* 4 (2017): 72–73.

Zhao, Yang. “ROBAM Electric Wang Qiang: Product research through research on cooking. (老板电器王强:通过研究[U+70F9][U+996A]来研究产品 in Chinese)” *Household Appliance* 10 (2017): 74–75.

CHAPTER 6

Standing Out in the Crowd in the B2B Market: A Success Story from Xinhai Technology Group

Yueqiu Hu, Shuning Zheng and Alain Yee Loong Chong

Introduction

Branding is one of the most important aspects of business strategy. In the current competitive and global market, branding can help companies achieve sustainable competitive advantage. A strong brand name works as a credible signal of product quality for imperfectly informed buyers and it is able to generate price premiums as a form of return to branding investments (Baltas and Saridakis 2010). Branding has been argued to be one of the most valuable assets for a company (Neumeier 2006). In a recent report by Forbes, the world's 100 most valuable brands are worth 2.15 trillion dollars. Not surprisingly, most of the world's most valuable brands are American companies such as Apple, Google, Amazon, and Coca Cola.

Y. Hu · S. Zheng · A. Y. L. Chong (✉)
University of Nottingham Ningbo China, Ningbo, China
e-mail: Alain.Chong@nottingham.edu.cn

Y. Hu
e-mail: Yueqiu.Hu@nottingham.edu.cn

M. J. Liu and J. Luo (eds.), *China Branding*,
https://doi.org/10.1007/978-981-13-9318-1_6

Despite China's growth into one of the largest economies in the world, Chinese brands have lagged behind other countries in achieving the same global impact.

One of the key reasons why Chinese brands have struggled to create brand names for themselves can be attributed to the fact that early Chinese manufacturers started their businesses from contract manufacturing and being original equipment manufacturers (OEMs) that competed based on lower cost rather than on innovation and design (Shepard 2016). However, with the focus on "Made in China" by the Chinese government, as well as greater emphasis on and investments in innovation and product design, Chinese companies such as Xiaomi and Huawei are starting to demonstrate how Chinese companies are catching up on the brand ladder. Recent studies conducted by Wu (2015) and Li and Guo (2012) have provided insights into how Chinese companies such as Tencent and Xiaomi are continuously employing branding strategies successfully. Despite some of the successes enjoyed by companies such as Tencent, Xiaomi, and others, there are still many Chinese manufacturers who are in the business-to-business (B2B) field that find it difficult to create brand awareness due to the limited opportunity to connect directly with their consumers.

In the business-to-customer (B2C) domain, the value of a brand is widely accepted by the marketers (Aaker 2009). In the field of B2B however, there is still limited attention being paid to the value of branding. In general, many manufacturers are still skeptical of the value that branding can offer (Leek and Christodoulides 2011). In B2C, efforts for brandings are usually invested into building emotional connections with the customers such as trust (Leek and Christodoulides 2012), whereas B2B manufacturers tend to focus more on the functional quality of their products. However, given the current competitive environment that manufacturers operate in, it is vital for them to have a strong brand value in order to gain a competitive advantage over their rivals.

In this paper, we present a case study on Xinhai Technology Group Co. Ltd. (hereafter, Xinhai) to demonstrate how a Chinese lighters and health-care equipments manufacturer is able to create its brand value in the B2B context, and subsequently become one of the largest lighter manufacturers in the world. A Revised Customer-Based Brand Equity (CBBE) model for B2B (Kuhn et al. 2008) provides the theoretical lens to help understand how branding is created by Xinhai. This case study provides useful strategies for Chinese B2B companies that would like to emulate the branding success of Xinhai.

Literature Review

Brand Equity

Branding refers to a set of marketing and communication methods that help to distinguish a company or its products from competitors, aiming to create a lasting impression in the minds of customers (Fahy and Jobber 2012). The word brand equity (Kim and Kim 2005) is used to measure the total value premium that a company generates from a product with a recognizable name, when compared to a generic equivalent. Kim and Kim (2005) employ three classifications of brand equity: consumer-based perspective, financial perspective, and comprehensive perspective, which incorporate the concepts of consumer-based brand equity and firm-based brand equity. Brand has the power to influence customer behavior; especially when markets become increasingly dynamic and are constantly fluctuating, it works as a marketing technique to increase customer satisfaction and customer loyalty, with side effects like reduced price sensitivity (Ghodeswar 2008; Srivastava and Thomas 2015).

Brand equity has received increasing interest from marketing researchers due to the growing need of systematic brands evaluation. It should be noted that brands are multidimensional with depth and breadth, length, scope, and density, and they also change and evolve continuously (Schultz 2015). For a strong brand, further facilitating brand and differentiating from competitors would be the key factors for corporates to consider (Krishnan 1996). The value will be an important means to attract and maintain customers. Innovation is a crucial part for both building and maintaining a strong brand (Aaker and Joachimsthaler 2012). Branding and product innovation are always interrelated and these two factors play a crucial role for obtaining customers' favorable impressions (Page and Herr 2002). A strong brand provides adequate resources for innovation and supports product launch. On the other hand, successful innovations also strengthen brand equity and improve brand profitability. Brexendorf et al. (2015) provide a framework in their paper showing the interdependency between brand and innovation. This framework contains three stages: brand provides guidance for innovation; brand supports launch of innovation, and successful innovation facilitates brand equity.

Keller et al. (2013) developed a CBBE Pyramid to assist management in their brand-building efforts. It is a four-step model that clarifies the way to build a strong brand. Firstly, brand identity must be ensured so that customers can associate with a specific product class or need when they see the brand. To do so, the goal of the first step is to create brand salience, thus, customers can recognize the brand and be aware of it. The second step is to establish brand meaning through strong, favorable, and unique brand associations. Specifically, the brand meaning can be created by combining performance and imagery. Performance contains functional factors such as product reliability and service effectiveness, which describes how well the product meets customers' needs. Imagery, on the other hand, is related to the extrinsic properties of the product, for example, user profiles, purchase, and usage situations, which place more emphasis on the intangible brand associations. The third step is brand response. According to Keller et al. (2013), customers' responses to the brand will fall into two categories, which are judgements and feelings. Customers will constantly make judgements about the brand and will emotionally respond to the brand according to how it makes them feel. In other words, the third step is to take account of customers' personal opinions that are based on both actual interaction or perceived reputation. Fourthly, brand resonance sits at the top of Keller's model. Resonance refers to the likelihood that a customer remains loyal to one brand. It can be achieved only when the customers feel a deep, psychological bond with the brand.

Customer-Based Brand Equity Framework

The CBBE model provides a yardstick by which brands can assess their progress in their brand-building efforts as well as guidance for marketing academies in their research. However, the model is focused primarily on an individual's perceptions of brands, which is not applicable for industrial buyers. In fact, B2B marketing also plays a significant part in the economy. It is reported by Kotler (2003) that B2B activity is 15 times greater than that in a B2C context. Brand equity also plays an important role. Scholars found that B2B buyers are willing to pay a premium price for their favorite brand due to the high brand equity, and are willing to recommend the brand to others (Bendixen et al. 2004; Ohnemus 2009). Successful examples are IBM, Cisco, and Intel, which have managed to build substantial equity and feature as the most valuable brands in the world (Interbrand 2017). Kuhn et al. (2008) examined Keller's consumer-based brand equity framework and extended the pyramid to a B2B context. Figure 6.1 presents the two models.

In Kuhn's revised model, salience, performance, and judgements are still applicable building blocks for the B2B context. Imagery is replaced by supplier reputation since the word is more appropriate to depict intangible attributes in an organizational context. Feelings are proved to be insignif-

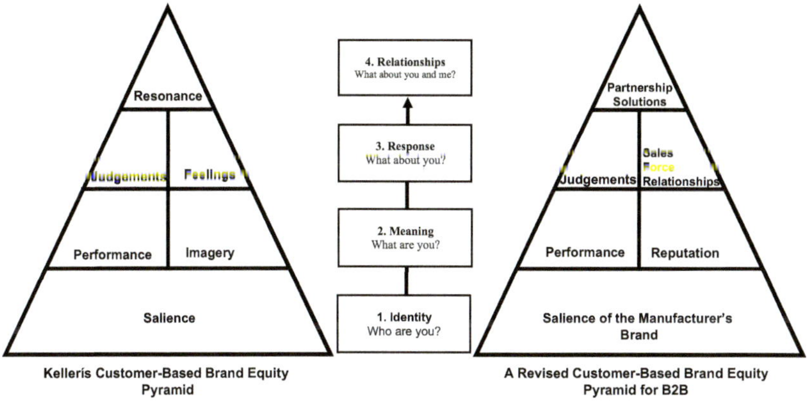

Fig. 6.1 Customer-based brand equity pyramids

icant in the B2B market while the purchase process is more rational than emotive. In addition, resonance is modified as well because for organizational buyers, behavioral loyalty may only appear to be a consequence of the contract period. Instead, company representatives play an important role in building brand equity, which indicates that further reinforcement should focus on buyer representatives and salespeople but not customers and brands.

Methodology

To study how B2B companies can successfully build their corporate brand value, we conducted a case study on a Chinese lighter manufacturing company—Xinhai Corporate, and developed a deep exploration into how their branding construction contributes value not just to customers, but also to employees, stakeholders, the environment, and a host of other ancillary factors that are too often ignored in today's fast-paced marketplace. We collected both primary interview data and secondary data on the company. In total, two-round group interviews have been conducted and all of the data were initially recorded and translated into English (Squires 2009). Thematic analysis was employed to analyze the transcribed interview data (Boyatzis 1998). The thematic interpretation coding follows Kuhn's revised CBBE model. When one author finished the first round code, the

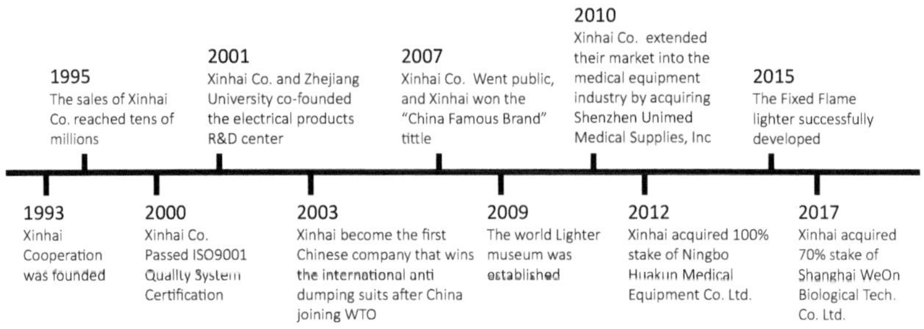

Fig. 6.2 History of Xinhai Co.

other co-authors worked as the devil's advocate by bringing forth alternative interpretations and counter-arguments to the coded themes until consensus (Adler and Adler 1988) was reached.

Case Study

Brief Introduction of the Xinhai Co.

Xinhai[1] was established in 1993 and is now one of the top three players in the global lighter industry. With the mission to become the world-class precision plastic manufacturer, Xinhai specializes in the development, manufacturing, and distribution of precise plastic products and medical equipments. Currently, Xinhai owns 9 subsidiary corporations and 4 manufacture bases. Figure 6.2 presents a brief summary of Xinhai's development history.

As the leader of the Chinese lighter industry, Xinhai is listed as one of the leading Chinese companies in terms of having the number of important trademarks. It is the first company in China that has children resistance (CR) technology that complies with the legal requirements from the European Union and is also the first company that participated in drafting China national safety standards for pocket lighters and utility lighters. Xinhai owns a national level Lighter Technology R&D Center and was the only company in the Chinese lighter industry to be awarded as a High-tech Innovation Company. Xinhai remains the largest lighter exporting company in China;

[1] Public Website: http://www.xinhaigroup.com/.

since 2000, 80% of their products are exported to more than 80 countries including the European Union, the United States, and Japan.

With 20 years experience in plastic mold manufacturing, besides producing and exporting lighters, in 2010 Xinhai entered the medical equipment domain. At present, Xinhai owns three medical equipment subsidiaries through independent innovation and acquisitions. In addition, Xinhai has set up 4 R&D centers in Ningbo, Shenzhen, Nanjing, and Shanghai. In 2017, Xinhai made around half their profits through the sales of medical equipment sections.

> Xinhai obtained an international lighter museum which contained over 25000 pieces of lighters. Xinhai's products is now exporting to over 80 countries. In the anti-dumping investigations, Xinhai played an important role. Xinhai participated in drafting two mandatory domestic lighter standards, and is the only Chinese firm joining in ISO International Safety Standard design. Researching for 8 years, a fixed flame lighter with AS materials came up in 2008. Now, Xinhai started a new journey in medical equipment domain. With huge capital and research investment, some nursing products attracted large amount attentions in industry and brought a new concept in medical equipment industry. (Vice President)

Xinhai's Brand Building Process

To Set up Brand Identity

After being regarded as an OEM and original design manufacturer (ODM) for several years, Xinhai shifted its focus to build a world-class lighter brand. Xinhai did not realize the importance of branding until encountering challenges from its franchisers. These franchisers registered the products designed by Xinhai and forced Xinhai to sell at a lower price. Consequently, in 1998, Xinhai set up an intellectual property department and registered and patented their own brand in 91 countries. Since 2010, Xinhai has extended its market in the medical equipment industry, and positioned itself as the expert manufacturer of the precision injection mold. They are now planning to create a new sub-branding for their medical equipment products, as explained by their vice president:

> We do not want to use Xinhai for medical equipment products due to the high brand awareness in lighter industry. When people talk about Xinhai, they will firstly associated with lighter, which make it strange when they see the medical equipment products. Thus, we want to create a new brand for

> medical equipment products- XINWELL. XINWELL would be the main brand for the medical equipment products, and we will also create sub-brand for different product lines according to their functions. (Vice President)

Instill Brand Value Through Actions
Xinhai has put in plenty of effort into building its brand culture. In 2009, after becoming one of the top three players in the lighter industry, Xinhai bought a lighter museum from the Netherlands Lighter Museum Foundation. They collected more than 25 thousand lighters from the Netherlands and translated the book, Legend of Lighter, to introduce the history of lighters. Picture 6.1 shows the internal environment of the lighter museum.

> Xinhai became a board member of international lighter museum foundation in 2007. Since that, the lighters in this museum can be exhibited in China. This foundation owned the largest collection and every lighter in the museum is unique. The museum acquired more than 25000 pieces of lighters and we can understand the popularization of ignition tool and other meaningful events from these… The president of Xinhai decided to translate this book to promote lighter culture and lighter industry and do something meaningful for the progress of human civilization. (Vice President)

The museum not only built Xinhai's brand culture externally, but it also assisted the company with its internal brand management. For the external advertising, this museum captures Xinhai's ambition in the industry, and helps to promote the lighter culture and industry. Meanwhile, Xinhai marketers are able to provide a historical overview of their products and educate their potential customers. Now visiting this lighter museum has become a regular routine for the factory's visitors. Internally, the museum has helped Xinhai to provide a strong sense of identity and helps employees to understand its mission and culture better. With these benefits, after stepping into the medical equipment industry, Xinhai also built two exhibition halls to show their medical equipments.

In addition, to achieve higher performance and generate better reputation, Xinhai remains open to innovation. By investing substantial capital and time in innovation, Xinhai not only achieves better revenue, but also extricates this firm from various difficult situations. To date, Xinhai has obtained 565 domestic patents and 32 international patents (Li and Wu 2011). In 2006, the Chinese National Bureau of Quality Supervision granted Xinhai the Chinese First Standard Innovation Contribution Award (Li and Wu 2011). Fixed flame valve is a typical example to show the achievement of

Picture 6.1 Lighter museum at Xinhai

Xinhai's innovation. Xinhai spent 10 years on developing the fixed flame lighter with AS material and this lighter has sold over one hundred million pieces. This invention also cut down the cost of manufacturing, which largely increases Xinhai's profitability. In the future, Xinhai will explore more in lighter inventions like utilizing degradable materials in developing its products.

Cooperation and Mergers

Cooperation is an important factor for Xinhai to accelerate their innovation. In 2009, Xinhai cooperated with Zhejiang University to establish a research center for developing a new lighter with CR (Xu and Zhu 2008). Besides that, Xinhai also continuously hires experts in the lighter industry to assist with their designs. Since 2001, Xinhai has invested more than 2 million dollars for introducing equipment from Switzerland and Germany and built an innovation team which contained more than 100 senior engineers including those from Japan and European countries (Shi 2014). Furthermore, in Xinhai's new business, the medical equipment, medical engineering cooperation will be the core point for further innovation. Since medical equipment is highly professional, it is almost impossible for a research center to design these products independently. Furthermore, the products by Xinhai also need to satisfy the doctors' needs. As remarked by the vice president from Xinhai:

> Hospital staffs are the most innovative on medical equipment. Doctors and nurses can generate idea when doing surgeries and taking care of patients. They can discover problems of the medical equipment, and generate ideas to solve the problems. However, applying these ideas are still unrealistic for doctors and nurses…Our advantage is that we can tell if this idea is applicable in manufacturing process. We can provide a sample in a very short time, so medical staffs can try it clinically. For hospital staffs, they can obtain their ideal medical tool, and for us, it is a great way to develop our new products. (Vice President)

Participate in Industry Standard Design

In September 2001, Xinhai attended the ISO TC61WG1 conference. They became the first Chinese enterprise that attended this conference and the implication of this event helped them to take the lead in modifying the international lighter standards (Xu and Zhu 2008). Xinhai is now gradually building their brand by attending more international conferences. Before entering the domestic market, Xinhai, as the head of the Chinese lighter industry, drafted Chinese lighters regulations with the Chinese government and tried to create a healthier business environment in the lighter domain. With these regulations, lighter firms will not be stuck in a price war but can focus on their products:

> We were thinking about selling in the domestic market. However, at that time, China has not set lighter standards. Thus, lighters with poor qualities can distribute in Chinese market well by taking price advantage. Thus, we decided to set up the lighter standards before entering domestic market. Without standard, we would all lose in the price war and it would be terrible for both customers and factories. Meanwhile, we would not accept to lower our quality which may ruin our international reputation. Therefore, we spent 6 years to design the Chinese lighter standards before entering domestic market. (Vice President)

Through these two means, Xinhai has clearly set their direction on how to be innovative. Innovation improves Xinhai as a brand. Concurrently, through the influence of the brand, Xinhai has created a better environment for innovation and understood the direction to innovate by joining in various design conferences.

Anti-dumping Investigations
When Xinhai gradually occupied the market share in foreign countries and threatened the interests of local firms, these firms gradually tried various means to mitigate the competition from Chinese lighter firms. In 1998, Xinhai finally won the Korean anti-dumping lawsuit. Korean tariff on lighters decreased from 112.8 to 72.41% and finally fell to 36.42% as a result of Xinhai's successful lawsuit (Liu 2016). After finishing the Korean anti-dumping case, in 2001, Xinhai was involved in the European anti-dumping investigation. With help from the Chinese ministry of commerce, Xinhai, along with other four manufacturers successfully proved that their exporting has not generated any harm to the lighter industry in European countries and successfully won the case.

Brand Extension
Xinhai is always a cautious and thoughtful investor. After turning into the top player in the lighter industry, Xinhai realized that they may eventually reach the ceiling for growth for the lighter industry and need to find a new market to further develop their firms. They analyzed the other lighter firms which successfully expanded their business to other industries and tried to

find Xinhai's core competence. After reviewing many industries, Xinhai learned the medical equipment market would be a good opportunity to expand their business since Xinhai is strong in precision plastic manufacturing. On the other hand, the medical equipment industry is also steadily growing but with few key manufacturers. When other private firms were still investing arbitrarily, Xinhai determined their strategic scheme and kept devoting efforts. Picture 6.2 shows medical equipment manufactured by Xinhai.

To find the insights of entering the new market, Xinhai investigated how other world-class lighter firms transformed their business models. The major competitor, BIC, expanded their market by producing disposable fast moving consumer goods (FMCG). They extended their brand from just a lighter manufacturer to the brand of products that people can associate with throughout their lifetime. Eventually, Xinhai decided to develop the new market through their core competitiveness.

> We investigated the transformation of other lighter firms like BIC and Swedish Match. The top lighter firm, BIC, expanding their products lines to other disposable plastic FMCG. Their idea is that customers can use BIC pens when they need to write, use BIC lighters when they need to smoke, and use BIC shavers when they need to shave. Another example is Swedish Match. They started their business from manufacturing matches. Then, they began their lighters business. After that, they entered tobacco industry, and now their lighter business only occupies less than 5% over the whole business. Surely it is very attracting but an impossible path in China. Thus, back to ourselves, we decided to find our core competence. (Vice President)

Xinhai penetrated the new market mainly through merger and acquisition. In 2008, Xinhai merged with a famous franchiser Unilite, and hired their manager as their own employee (Liu 2009). The cautious investment approach helped Xinhai adapt to the new market in a relatively quick manner. With the mission to become a leading medical equipment supplier, Xinhai acquired Unimed Medical Supplies Inc., Ningbo Huakun Medical Equipment Co. Ltd., Ningbo GeePi Bio-Instrument Co. Ltd., and Shanghai WeOn Biological Technology Co. Ltd., subsequently.

> Firstly, we merged Unimed in Shenzhen. We purchased 20% share of this firm for being conscious. With more understanding on this firm and the whole industry, we then purchased 51% share. Finally, we purchased the whole company. After that, we also purchased Huakun in Ningbo and moved their man-

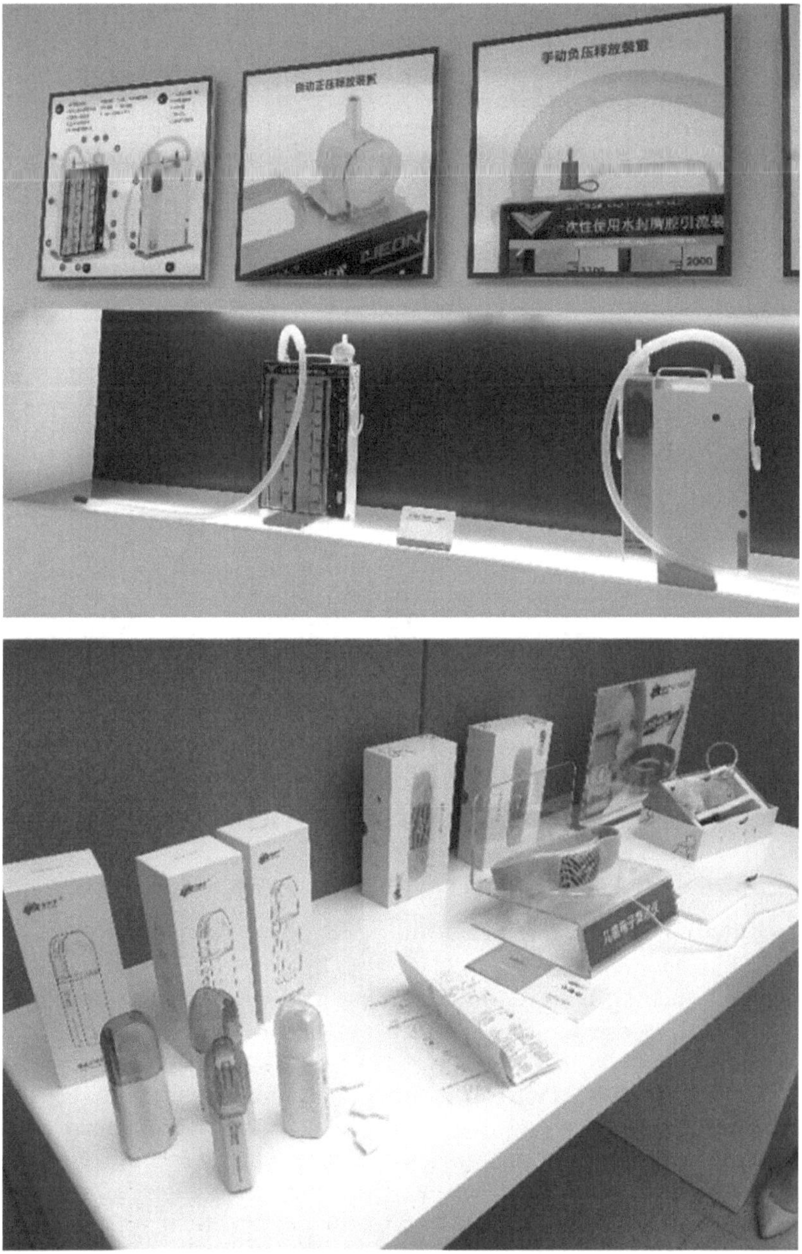

Picture 6.2 Medical equipment samples from Xinhai

> ufacture from Ninghai to Cixi… Most talents in medical industry are staying in Shenzhen and Shanghai so we brought the firm in Shenzhen… Though merging a company in Shenzhen, we still want to put medical equipment manufacture here (Cixi). We can build research center in Shanghai and Shenzhen, but for factory, we want to build in here. Thus, we merged the Huakun corporate and hope the staffs in headquarter can learn more about medical equipment industry. (Vice President)

As a lighter manufacturer, Xinhai have extended their brand horizontally when introducing medical equipment to the market since the medical equipment market is different from the lighter market. Understanding that there is a risk of product cannibalization as the new brand may compete with the core brand, Xinhai merged two medical equipment brands and created a new brand called XINWELL for medical equipment (Chen and Liu 2004).

> In the medical equipment business, we intend to create a new brand instead of Xinhai, because Xinhai is famous in the lighter industry. When people mention Xinhai, they will automatically associate with lighters. Thus, people will felt weird when heading Xinhai medical equipment… Overall, we decided to create a new brand called XINWELL. XINWELL will be the major brand for medical equipment business. (Vice President)

Currently, Unimed and Huakun already obtain leading positions in the medical equipment business. Unimed currently has 140 million sales per year and is a key source of revenue for Xinhai. On the other hand, Huakun has reached 4 million sales but is growing fast.

Discussion and Implication

Table 6.1 provides a summary of Xinhai's branding development process. From initially setting up brand identity to brand extension into different fields, the finding has revealed a number of dimensions that should be considered when manufacturers want to build their brands in the B2B context.

Firstly, innovation is the source of power for brand construction. Keeping innovation will not only improve the brand's reputation, but also assist in maintaining a strong customer loyalty with organizational buyers. Apart from taking reference from advanced products from competitors, companies should assist in investing in research and development in order to create core competitive advantages.

Table 6.1 Summary of Xinhai's branding development process

Setting up brand identity	*Instill brand value through actions*	*Brand extensions*
• Shift from low cost to a company that is known to be open to ideas, innovative, and has a strong sense of community and integrity • Setting up IP department and applying for patents in order to differentiate their products from others • Moving from just being a lighter manufacturer to a manufacturer that is innovative (moving into healthcare equipment manufacturing)	• To instill branding value that customers/partners can associate with (e.g. building a museum that introduces the history of lighters and the company) • The company demonstrates its brand identity by addressing the issues related to CR, where it invests time and money to come up with a product that complies with the standards • The company also further builds its reputation as a company that has a strong sense of community and integrity by participating in the anti-dumping case, as well as participating in setting up industrial standards	• Entering new markets but with the same brand values • Entering into the medical equipment industry and using the same brand identity that has been established for their lighter company • Consistent branding efforts for both operations of lighter and medical equipment

Besides, for a strong brand, further facilitating the brand and differentiating it from competitors by constructing special corporate culture would be an instructive way for corporates to consider. As supported by Bocock (2008) not in reference list, consumption is not just an economic process but a social and cultural process involving cultural symbolism. Creating a unique corporate culture will not only enhance enterprise cohesion, but also increase trust among industrial partners, thus maintaining a stable long-term relationship.

Furthermore, firm managers should think a step ahead on every decision. What the brand is today or what it was yesterday is less important than what it might be tomorrow. The brand managers need to think of tomorrow and beyond with a dynamic view that covers multidimensional consideration (Schultz 2015). Managers should be sensitive to market changes and be vigilant for corporate crises and emergencies.

In addition, when there is a brand extension, companies should select the brand architecture cautiously according to the actual situation. Although it is desired to enter new markets that share the same mission with the company, it is not necessary to use the same brand. In that case, creating a sub-brand may be better for maintaining brand image consistency.

Limitations and Future Research

This research is not without limitation. Firstly, our study focused on the company side of branding construction; there is an absence of organizational customer's confirmation. Secondly, in our case study, the company Xinhai, as a plastic equipment manufacturer, produces their main products such as lighters and plastic medical equipment. All of these products belong to fast-moving consumer goods, which only contribute to a part of the whole market. This represents future research opportunities. Firstly, future research can extend our work by adding organizational customers' side evidences. In addition, there is a need for further effort to validate the findings in different industrial marketing contexts.

Further Investigation

1. What is Xinhai's plan for their future brand extension?
2. What are the other actions that Xinhai could take for instilling brand value?
3. How can a brand decide that they need transformation?

References

Aaker, David A. *Managing brand equity*. New York, NY: Simon & Schuster, 2009.

Aaker, David A., and Erich Joachimsthaler. *Brand leadership*. New York, NY: Simon & Schuster, 2012.

Adler, Patricia A., and Peter Adler. "Intense loyalty in organizations: A case study of college athletics." *Administrative Science Quarterly* 33, no. 3 (1988): 401–417.

Baltas, George, and Charalampos Saridakis. "Measuring brand equity in the car market: A hedonic price analysis." *Journal of the Operational Research Society* 61, no. 2 (2010): 284–293.

Bendixen, Mike, Kalala A. Bukasa, and Russell Abratt. "Brand equity in the business-to-business market." *Industrial Marketing Management* 33, no. 5 (2004): 371–380.

Bocock, R. *Consumption*. London: Routledge, 2008.

Boyatzis, Richard E. *Transforming qualitative information: Thematic analysis and code development*. Thousand Oaks, CA: Sage, 1998.

Brexendorf, Tim Oliver, Barry Bayus, and Kevin Lane Keller. "Understanding the interplay between brand and innovation management: Findings and future research directions." *Journal of the Academy of Marketing Science* 43, no. 5 (2015): 548–557.

Chen, Kuang-Jung, and Chu-Mei Liu. "Positive brand extension trial and choice of parent brand." *Journal of Product & Brand Management* 13, no. 1 (2004): 25–36.

Fahy, John, and David Jobber. *Foundations of marketing*. London: McGraw-Hill Higher Education, 2012.

Ghodeswar, Bhimrao M. "Building brand identity in competitive markets: a conceptual model." *Journal of Product & Brand Management* 17, no. 1 (2008): 4–12.

Interbrand. "Best Global Brand 2017." https://www.interbrand.com/best-brands/best-global-brands/2017/.

Keller, Kevin Lane, M. G. Parameswaran, and Isaac Jacob. *Strategic brand management: Building, measuring, and managing brand equity*. Upper Saddle River, NJ: Pearson Education, 2013.

Kim, Hong-bumm, and Woo Gon Kim. "The relationship between brand equity and firms' performance in luxury hotels and chain restaurants." *Tourism Management* 26, no. 4 (2005): 549–560.

Kotler, Philip. *Marketing management*. 11th ed. Upper Saddle River, NJ: Prentice Hall, 2003.

Krishnan, H. Shanker. "Characteristics of memory associations: A consumer-based brand equity perspective." *International Journal of Research in Marketing* 13, no. 4 (1996): 389–405.

Kuhn, Kerri-Ann L., Frank Alpert, and Nigel K. Ll Pope. "An application of Keller's brand equity model in a B2B context." *Qualitative Market Research: An International Journal* 11, no. 1 (2008): 40–58.

Leek, Sheena, and George Christodoulides. "A literature review and future agenda for B2B branding: Challenges of branding in a B2B context." *Industrial Marketing Management* 40, no. 6 (2011): 830–837.

Leek, Sheena, and George Christodoulides. "A framework of brand value in B2B markets: The contributing role of functional and emotional components." *Industrial Marketing Management* 41, no. 1 (2012): 106–114.

Li, Binwei, and Ruolan Wu. "Using technology to expanding market." *Ningbo Communication Journal*, no. 10 (2011): 35.

Li, Sainan, and Fangfang Guo. "The development road of a successful brand: A case study of Tencent QQ." Student thesis, 2012.

Liu, Gang. "Xinhai's international mergers." *Chinese Hardware Journal*, no. 5 (2009): 58.

Liu, Zhaoyong. "Discussing how Chinese exporting firm responding anti-dumping investigation: Using Xinihai's anti-dumping investigations as examples." *The Chinese Economist*, no. 6 (2016): 92.

Neumeier, Marty. "The brand gap: How to bridge the distance between business strategy and design." Berkeley, CA: New Riders, Pearson Education, 2006.

Ohnemus, Lars. "B2B branding: A financial burden for shareholders?" *Business Horizons* 52, no. 2 (2009): 159–166.

Page, Christine, and Paul M. Herr. "An investigation of the processes by which product design and brand strength interact to determine initial affect and quality judgments." *Journal of Consumer Psychology* 12, no. 2 (2002): 133–147.

Schultz, Don E. "Rethinking brand development in an interactive marketplace." In *The future of branding*, edited by Gregory M. Thomas and Rajendra K. Srivastava, 199. New Delhi, India: Sage, 2015.

Shepard, Wade. "The revolutionary rise of the Chinese brand." *Forbes*, 2016.

Shi, Xiaoxuan. "One step ahead: Xinhai as leading firm in lighter industry." *China Inspection and Quarantine Journal*, no. 6 (2014): 30–32.

Squires, Allison. "Methodological challenges in cross-language qualitative research: A research review." *International Journal of Nursing Studies* 46, no. 2 (2009): 277–287.

Srivastava, Rajendra K., and Gregory M. Thomas. *The future of branding*. New Delhi, India: Sage, 2015.

Wu, Fang-Fang. "Discussion on brand marketing culture of Xiaomi phone." *Prices Monthly*, 2015.

Xu, Xu, and Yunwei Zhu. "Innovation to win the international competition." *Technology Management Research Journal* 28, no. 9 (2008): 23–25.

CHAPTER 7

Crafting a Successful Business Strategy: A Case of Zhejiang Yinlun Machinery Co. Ltd.

M. S. Balaji

Introduction

In today's marketplace, characterized by intense local and global competition, crafting a successful business strategy is vital to the success of any organization. Crafting a business strategy is the process of exploiting an organization's resources and competencies to meet both short-term and long-term objectives and achieve marketplace success. This exploitation of resources and competencies depends on the strategy or the course of action the organization pursues drawing on the market sensing and understanding customers and value created for them. Crafting a business strategy is much more than developing a plan and chasing it. It involves the interplay between the market conditions, customer expectations, and the competition, where the organization decides the course of action to pursue and acts in a coordinated way to meet its objectives and goals. As business success depends on delivering superior value to customers, the most important

M. S. Balaji (✉)
University of Nottingham Ningbo China, Ningbo, China
e-mail: SathyaprakashBalaji.Makam@nottingham.edu.cn

M. J. Liu and J. Luo (eds.), *China Branding*,
https://doi.org/10.1007/978-981-13-9318-1_7

strategic decision in crafting a successful business strategy involves choosing the customers to serve and understanding how organizations can create superior value for its customer. This involves understanding what an organization does or is proficient in doing and what resources will the organization have to invest in across its functional areas to be able to deliver superior customer value and achieve marketplace success. We discuss this process of crafting business strategy through the discussion of Yinlun Co. Ltd., a leading automobile parts and machine tools company in China.

Zhejiang Yinlun Machinery Co. Ltd., was founded in 1958 as a local state-owned machinery factory in Tiantia and focused initially on manufacturing agricultural machine tools including rice threshers, rice transplanters, rice scourers, flour mills, diesel machines, water turbine pumps, and others. During the financial difficulties experienced in the late 1980s and early 1990s, it merged with six local enterprises engaged in auto parts, industrial machinery, papermaking, cement, and radio making businesses as Zhejiang Tiantai Machinery Factory. In the mid and later 1990s, the company started focusing on developing oil coolers and by 1998, its annual sales reached RMB 39.56 million with foreign exchange earning of USD 20 million. In 1999, the company changed its name to Zhejiang Yinlun Machinery Co. Ltd., and was formally established with the approval of the Zhejiang Administration for Industry and Commerce. During the late 1990s, it focused on developing aluminum intercoolers and tube-fin coolers. In 2007, the company was listed on the small and medium board of the Shenzhen Stock Exchange. In 2008, the company undertook to develop the "National Torch Program Project" and set about developing cutting-edge products and technologies in automotive parts and machine tools. In 2011, the company invested into the front-end module of automobile and machinery cooling modules, which laid the foundation for sustainable development in the 12th five year-plan period. It has won many awards, and today it is a world-class heat exchanger expert and has evolved into an industry leader in oil, water, and gas heat exchangers. In 2017, its sales increased to RMB 4.2 billion with its business expanded into fields including agricultural machinery, compressors, wind power generation, generator sets, train locomotives, and industrial heat exchangers. While the domestic market contributes 65% of its revenue, the remaining 35% comes from its global operations. It is the biggest oil cooler producer in the world and has about 3000 employees worldwide. Its key customers include Caterpillar, Cummins, WeiChai, Geely, Yu, Great Wall, and XCMG, among others.

Today, it is one of the biggest OEM companies in China and is considered as a Zhejiang Outstanding Enterprise.

The remainder of the article is structured as follows. We discuss how the market strategy is crafted which forms the basis for understanding Yinlun's business strategy. The case analysis and the discussion are presented next followed by the challenges faced by the company and the conclusion.

Business Strategy

Strategy is considered an important determinant of business performance. Porter (1996) in his seminal work "What is Strategy?" suggests that many firms fail to differentiate between strategy and operational excellence. While operational excellence involves performing similar activities as competitors in a better way, strategy, on the other hand, involves performing a different set of activities from competitors or performing a similar set of activities differently. Bracker (1980) states that strategy involves significant programs of actions that are performed to reach the organizational goals and objectives. This involves the allocation and coordination of resources in meeting the organizational goals. Taken together, the strategy is about identifying the course of action an organization pursues that generates superior value to customers and the stakeholders by efficient use of its resources and competencies. Because strategy is a fundamental course of action that an organization pursues, Porter (1996) contends that it would provide a competitive advantage and ensure business success. Business strategy as an overarching strategy brings together various other strategies including marketing strategy, technology strategy, and financial strategy (Teece 2010). As business strategy views organizations as the value-generating enterprise, we rely on value-based strategies to understand how Zhejiang Yinlun Machinery Co. Ltd., allocates and coordinates various resources in various activities that generate superior value to its customers and achieve marketplace success.

Value-Based Strategies

At the core of a successful business strategy is understanding what customers regard as superior value and how firms can provide this superior value to customers. While prior literature offers several fundamental strategies that enable firms to offer superior value to its customers, Treacy and Wiersema (1993) consolidate them into three major strategies, namely operational excellence, product excellence, and customer excel-

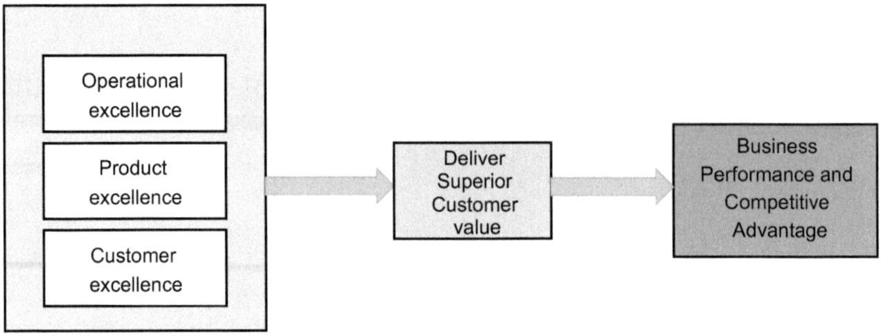

Fig. 7.1 Value-based strategies and business performance

lence. Figure 7.1 presents the value-based strategies and how they guide an organization in crafting a successful business strategy.

Operational Excellence

Operational excellence refers to offering customers reliable products and services of reasonable quality and low price against competitive price and convenience (Hoogeweegen et al. 2006). Operational excellence seeks operating efficacy by reducing errors and providing high-quality products or services at the best total cost to customers. In other words, operational excellence emphasizes value-for-money. An operationally excellent organization would organize to provide their high-quality offering to a specific or defined set of customers at the lowest cost. For operationally excellent organizations, the primary focus is on production and operations processes and maintaining good relations with its suppliers (Tallon 2007). Operational excellence is different from operational effectiveness. While operational effectiveness involves performing similar activities as competitors in a better way, operational excellence involves doing different activities from competitors that enable organizations to provide better products than competitors at a low cost.

Operational excellence is a broader program that involves improving and sustaining business performance in which quality and value are embedded. Operational excellence also involves other excellence concepts such as service excellence, manufacturing excellence, and supply chain excellence. Operational excellence is a long journey that involves (1) meeting the objectives of operations management, (2) establishing a competitive advantage,

(3) achieving business leadership, and (4) sustaining operational excellence (Basu 2004). Thus, operational excellence is a mindset that emphasizes sustainable improvement in business processes. Furthermore, it is evident that both quality management and continuous improvement are integral to operational excellence.

Product Excellence

Product excellence or product leadership refers to "offering customers leading-edge products and services that consistently enhance the customers' use or application of the product, thereby making rivals goods obsolete" (Treacy and Wiersema 1993, 91). Organizations that pursue product excellence emphasize continuous innovation and relentlessly focus on improving the product or service. In its pursuit of product excellence, the organization may seek out technologies from other industries that would enable it to solve problems creatively or to enhance its products or services further. Furthermore, organizations that pursue product excellence will try to offer a product that delivers the best performance in the market and would seek to obsolete its products before its competitor does. The organization pursuing product excellence will rely on its experience and learning to innovate new products at lower costs.

Organizations that pursue product leadership must focus on functionality, features, and performance of its products and services. According to Beatty and Schneier (1997), organizations competing on product excellence emphasize innovation in products and services and create competitive advantage. They would seek employees who have an entrepreneurial mindset, are driven by learning, and committed to working as a team (Ulrich 1998). Organizations pursuing product excellence can also adopt a variety-based positioning in that they can focus on producing a range of products that are outstanding for a particular segment of customers.

Customer Excellence

Customer excellence refers to having an in-depth understanding of the target consumer needs and tailoring the products and services to match the demands of the target customers. It involves segmenting customers precisely and identifying a target market to tailor the offering to match with the targeted customers' needs (Akçura and Srinivasan 2005). An organization that pursues customer excellence recognizes that retaining customers

Table 7.1 The description of the three value-based strategies

Value-based strategies	*Operational excellence*	*Product excellence*	*Customer excellence*
Core activity	Operating efficiency	Continuous innovation of product	Tailoring customer needs with products
Value proposition	Low cost—reduce total cost	Best product—high quality product	Best solution—matching needs with solution
Strategic focus	High quality product at low price—emphasize value-for-money	Innovate faster and relentless focus on improving products and services	Better understand customer needs and maintain close customer relationships

is more profitable and would emphasize building a long-term relationship with its customers. By building a sustainable relationship with its customers, organizations can better understand customers' requirements and improve their product to adapt to customers' needs at a lower cost. This reduces the cost of serving the customers as well as increasing their profitability (Osei 2017). Moreover, by developing a close relationship with its customers, they can better foresee the changes in customer preference, and this will enable them to be better prepared to serve customers in both the short-term and long-term. Also, organizations pursuing customer excellence can develop an in-depth understanding of its customers' needs and this might aid organizations to broaden their business by cross-selling other products or services with those customers. Thus, customer excellence can result in a personalized customer experience, which can increase loyalty and increase return-on-investments.

Customer excellence strategies include increasing customer touchpoints which could provide more opportunities for the customers to interact with an organization (Dhebar 2013). Other strategies include customer service management, which involves providing consistent and quick responses to customers in handling queries or service complaints. As customers engage with an organization through several channels, companies can use data integration systems to gain an in-depth understanding of its customers, fine-tune its segments, and offer a more focused and personalized campaign to strengthen the relationship with its customers (Table 7.1).

We argue that organizations can pursue organizational excellence, product excellence, and customer excellence in delivering superior customer value, which in turn, results in increased business performance and development of a competitive advantage. We present the case of Zhejiang Yinlun Machinery Co. Ltd., and its value-based strategies in establishing it as a leading automobile parts and machine tools company in China.

Analysis and Discussion of Yinlun's Business Strategy

Since being founded 50 years ago, Yinlun Co. Ltd., today is a global firm with a presence in several countries in Asia, Europe, and the United States. As a leader in China's automobile radiators, Yinlun is currently focusing on international markets to establish it as a global leader in heat exchangers and other machine and tools sectors. This is reflected in its vision of being a respected company in the field of heat exchange and post-treatment. Its strategy focuses on four internationalization pillars of product, talent, manufacturing, and management. It aims to achieve excellence in operations, customers, and products to become a global leader.

Yinlun Business System

Yinlun's operational excellence is based on the Yinlun Business System (YBS), which is based on the philosophies of "excellence" and "continuous improvement." YBS is a company-wide strategy that involves all functional departments aiming to improve customer satisfaction. Though YBS is based on the lean manufacturing concepts such as 6sigma, QSB, 8D, 7-step, and CBS, it includes other business operations including strategic planning, human resource management, product development, and customer service. In short, it covers all aspects of business operations. The starting point of YBS is customer value and satisfaction which aims to realize the virtuous circle of creating value for its shareholders, customers, and employees. The two unique features of YBS are the corporate culture and identity and decision process. The corporate culture and identity describes Yinlun's business model and its strategy. This covers both the business environment and company environment where the strategy development and implementation consider both environments. The second feature is the decision process where it follows a top–down approach. The top management provides the strategic direction and resources for meeting the organization's goals and objectives. This is reflected in Yinlun's 15 guiding principles and manual which are linked with the enterprise spirit and corporate culture.

Product Strategy

Yinlun's product excellence is based on innovation and relentless focus on improving product quality. It follows a product portfolio strategy and manufactures several products including oil coolers, stainless steel oil coolers, aluminum oil coolers, copper oil coolers, cooling modules, air coolers, water air coolers, heat sinks, commercial vehicle cooling modules, car front-end modules, die casting, EGR, and SCR systems. It manufactures more than 3000 varieties of products used in engines, gearboxes, mechanics, hydraulic systems, air conditioning, and refrigeration. These products are used in automobiles, construction machinery, agricultural machinery, train locomotives, wind turbines, ships, and civil applications. It is the market leader in oil coolers and intercoolers with 45 and 35% market share. Yinlun's success in product excellence is built on continuous innovation. In its strive to excel, it built a joint R&D center with Zhejiang University, Shanghai Jiaotong University, Harbin Institute of Technology, and Zhejiang Science and Technology Institute and established a long-term cooperation with the Internal Combustion Engine Research Institute of China, Tsinghua University, AVL Research Institute in Austria, and Lakoff Research Institute in Russia as well as many other universities and research institutes around the world.

Besides research collaborations, Yinlun has set up national post-doctoral research institutions where it employs more than 200 research students. It also set up a heat exchanger test center which is the largest of its type in China. Yinlun invests about 4% of its revenue in R&D and possesses more than 80 patents. Furthermore, it sets high-level benchmarks based on customer requirements, peers, and leading companies in China and global markets. Some of its key benchmark indicators include product defects, sales, manufacturing cost, product specifications, and production efficiency. It has successfully been certified by ISO 9002, QS9000, VDA 6.1 as well as ISO/TS 16949, ISO 14001, and OHSAA18001. As customer requirements are changing, Yinlun strives to produce world-class and high-quality products and aims to turn Yinlun into a world-class supplier of automobile parts and machine tools company and become a top player in the global market.

Customer Intimacy

Yinlun's customer excellence revolves around the in-depth understanding of client needs and developing products that closely meet their clients' needs. As Yinlun's products are varied and include clients from the United States, Europe, Asia, and China markets, it focuses on developing a personal relationship with its clients. As YBS starts with customer satisfaction, Yinlun has a strong commitment to understanding client needs, and as part of this often conducts "technical day," where they invite individual clients and showcase their innovations and products to seek feedback from the clients. Furthermore, they often seek feedback from clients regarding their products and use this information for product improvements. It spent about RMB 20 million in 2017 on marketing activities. This has enabled Yinlun to retain its clients and attract new ones over the last decade.

Challenges

While Yinlun is able to offer high-quality products at low customer cost, a key challenge it faces in fulfilling its vision is building its brand in the global market. Brands and brand building are of growing interest in business markets. While in business markets, brands may have no inherent meaning, it becomes endowed through its performance as the supplier and its market offering over time. While various Yinlun products such as oil coolers and intercoolers may deliver superior functionality and performance to its clients, developing a strong brand name may become an important resource for its clients in the global markets. So, a key challenge Yinlun faces is developing a brand strategy that reflects its products' superior functionality and performance to its clients.

A second challenge Yinlun faces is managing its product portfolio. While oil coolers and intercoolers are top performing products for Yinlun in both domestic and global markets, it has a plethora of other products across different categories. Managing many products in the portfolio may result in reduced forecasting accuracy, increased operations, marketing, and R&D costs, confused clients and channel partners, increased inventory-related costs, and may impact revenue and the cost of the product over its life cycle. Also, managing many products may result in a negative aspect such as weak strategy development and might lead to a lack of consistent interest and understanding of clients. The organizational design and management practices may be affected by many product portfolio strategies and also it might limit the availability of organizational resources for all products.

A third key challenge for Yinlun is its internationalization strategy. While Yinlun has invested significant resources in R&D centers around the world, a key challenge involves the international company structure, global pricing strategy, and worldwide environmental issues. Furthermore, with cultural differences and communication difficulties, effective communication across its clients, employees, and partners is needed for internationalization success.

Conclusion

Crafting a successful business strategy is vital to business performance and success. We suggest that a successful business strategy hinges on developing value-based strategies such as product excellence, operational excellence, and customer excellence that deliver superior client value and business performance. Through the case of Zhejiang Yinlun Machinery Co. Ltd., we show that an in-depth understanding of client needs and focusing on customer satisfaction enables them to consistently develop high-quality products that closely meet client needs.

Further Investigation

1. How can Yinlun build a strong brand for global business markets?
2. What product portfolio management strategy should Yinlun follow for achieving product excellence?
3. What marketing activities should Yinlun engage into increase customer intimacy and customer satisfaction?

References

Akçura, M. Tolga, and Kannan Srinivasan. "Research note: Customer intimacy and cross-selling strategy." *Management Science* 51, no. 6 (2005): 1007–1012.

Basu, Ron. *Implementing quality: A practical guide to tools and techniques: Enabling the power of operational excellence*. Cengage Learning EMEA, 2004.

Beatty, Richard W., and Craig Eric Schneier. "New HR roles to impact organizational performance: From 'partners' to 'players'." *Human Resource Management (1986–1998)* 36, no. 1 (1997): 29.

Bracker, Jeffrey. "The historical development of the strategic management concept." *Academy of Management Review* 5, no. 2 (1980): 219–224.

Dhebar, Anirudh. "Toward a compelling customer touchpoint architecture." *Business Horizons* 56, no. 2 (2013): 199–205.

Hoogeweegen, Martijn R., Diederik W. van Liere, Peter H. M. Vervest, Lorike Hagdorn van der Meijden, and Ido de Lepper. "Strategizing for mass customization by playing the business networking game." *Decision Support Systems* 42, no. 3 (2006): 1402–1412.

Osei, Godfred. "Customer intimacy adoption and its impact on organisational performance." *Journal of Research in Marketing* 8, no. 1 (2017): 600–616.

Porter, Michael E. "What is strategy." *Harvard Business Review* 74, no. 6 (1996): 61–78.

Tallon, Paul P. "A process-oriented perspective on the alignment of information technology and business strategy." *Journal of Management Information Systems* 24, no. 3 (2007): 227–268.

Teece, David J. "Business models, business strategy and innovation." *Long Range Planning* 43, no. 2–3 (2010): 172–194.

Treacy, Michael, and Fred Wiersema. "Customer intimacy and other value disciplines." *Harvard Business Review* 71, no. 1 (1993): 84–93.

Ulrich, Dave. "A new mandate for human resources." *Harvard Business Review* 76 (1998): 124–135.

CHAPTER 8

Weixing: A Plastic Pipe Industry Leader Who Succeeded with Manufacturing Upgrading and Long-Term R&D Investment

Cherry Yi Zhang and Tiantian Zhang

Industry Background

Slower economic growth, China–USA trade friction, and real estate regulation have revealed a pessimistic outlook for potential downstream customers of the plastic pipe industry. Although domestic construction may regain its spotlight due to international trade friction, strong government regulations make the growth of the real estate sector uncertain; as an upstream supplier in the real estate sector, this pessimistic outlook has also spilled over to the plastic pipe industry due to the potential loss of sales. Because of this slower growth, technologies and services upgrading are expected to be the new direction for the industry to survive. The raw material costs in the plastic pipe industry are strongly connected to the eco-

C. Y. Zhang (✉) · T. Zhang
University of Nottingham Ningbo China, Ningbo, China
e-mail: Cherry-Yi.Zhang@nottingham.edu.cn

T. Zhang
e-mail: Tiantian.Zhang@nottingham.edu.cn

M. J. Liu and J. Luo (eds.), *China Branding*,
https://doi.org/10.1007/978-981-13-9318-1_8

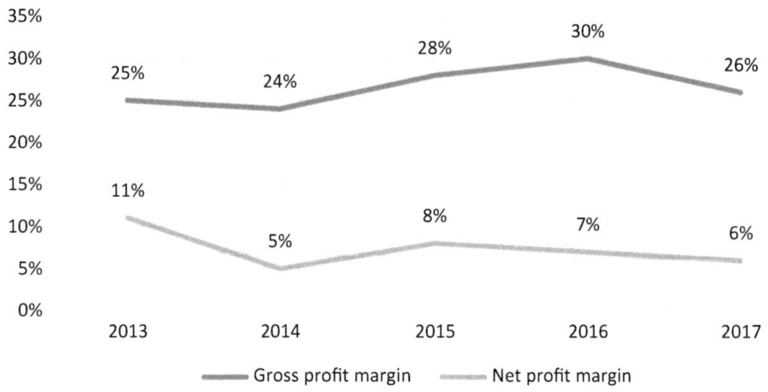

Fig. 8.1 Industry gross profit margin and net profit margin

nomic cycle and the political risk in the oil producing countries. In 2018, political risk induced higher oil prices, and environmental costs increased the industry's cost of production. Production line upgrading to improve production efficiency may help companies to win a larger market share in this industry downturn. Figure 8.1 shows the trend of the industry gross profit margin and net profit margin from 2013 to 2017; both profit margins dropped in the year 2017.

Location bias is strong in the plastic pipe industry in China. Customer preference varies geographically. Currently, the distribution channel of the products still follows the old business model. In the future, the growth of pipe companies depends on the added value of the "service" component and the logistics network upgrading.

Company Background

Relative to its peer firms, as a leading company in the plastic pipe industry established in 1999, Zhejiang Weixing New Bldg Mtls Co. Ltd. (Weixing) moved one-step ahead and established a strong logistics network by strategically locating the production units and upgrading their technology. The company firmly aligns its strategy of "retailing led value chain penetration" and has expanded its business into three areas: household retailing, commercial real estate projects, and government funded infrastructure projects. Weixing invests heavily in research and development. With a strong focus

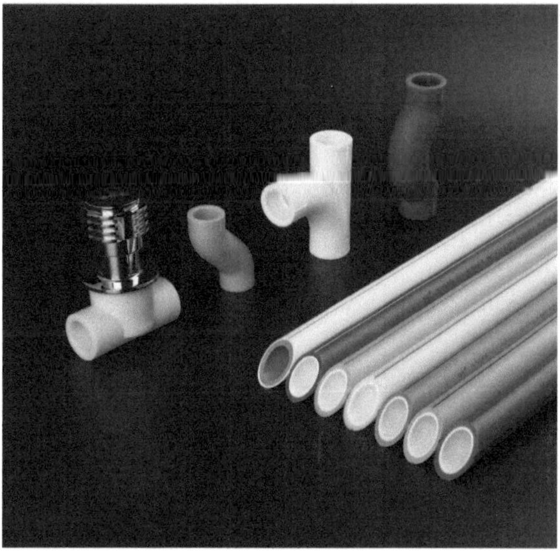

Picture 8.1 Weixing's pipe

on product quality, their three major brands, Weixing Tube (pipe), Annette (water purifier), and Kale (waterproof paint) are able to sell at a premium (Picture 8.1).

Weixing has five major modern manufacturing plants strategically located in Zhejiang, Shanghai, Tianjin, Chongqing, and Xi'an, all with strong research and development strengths. The geographical barrier indicates that their competitors are isolated by geographical factors, therefore, there are few competitive enterprises across the country, and those leading enterprises with strong bargaining power will be able to impose discipline through devices like price leadership (Porter 1980). Weixing produces three types of pipeline products: PPR pipes are designed for cold and hot water supply in buildings primarily sold through domestic retailing channels; PE and PVC pipes are used in the infrastructural projects including plumbing, heating, gas, culvert systems, and other fields, with target customers in government and real estate developers. The company succeeded with a strategy of brand recognition through retailing. Benefitting from the retailing channel, the brand value of Weixing has now spilled over to large sales and evolved into a major supplier of big real estate and government development projects.

Related Literature

Research on product uncertainty is based on agency theory. The agency theory applies to all types of transactions where information asymmetry exists. In a purchasing transaction, buyers are viewed as principals that delegate the agents (sellers) the delivery of the promised product quality. The sellers are viewed as agents because they typically have more information about the products. The uncertainty of the received product arises since the buyer does not have the complete information and cannot fully assess the seller's quality, leading to adverse selection (Akerlof 1978; Pavlou et al. 2007; Dimoka et al. 2012).

Products with low visibility like pipes will have product uncertainty that originated from information asymmetry and led to adverse selection. As suggested by Pavlou et al. (2007), seller reputation and trust in sellers partially mitigate this uncertainty. Moreover, the seller's brand's historical positive records could reduce the uncertainty of the perceived risk in the purchasing transaction.

The literature on information asymmetry concludes that buyers with biased information are dissatisfied and they discount prices they are willing to pay (Milgrom and Weber 1982). This makes it difficult for sellers with historically perceived low-quality products to charge premium prices, but may enable sellers with a high product quality reputation to charge the premium prices.

The research has also investigated the signals that could be adopted as the mechanisms to reduce the problem of adverse selection. Signals are the actions that sellers take to reveal their true type. Kirmani and Rao (2000) review the ways that managers use to signal the unobservable product quality. In Kirmani and Rao (2000), quality signals can be recognized through many ways, including brand name, price, warranty, and advertising expenditures. Specifically, brand names allow unobservable quality to be communicated, as the sellers need long-term commitment and expenditure to build brand equity. The cost of building the brand must be revealed from future increased sales. A low-quality seller will not be able to sustain the investment in the brand as the sales will not increase after the low quality is revealed. Similarly, the ability of keeping the high price in a competitive market can also be a sign of good quality. Moreover, Hendricks and

Singhal (1996) show that the firm market value enhances when it wins quality awards; this indicates that a firm can use the quality awards to signal or communicate with its current and potential customers regarding the product quality.

Management literature also broadly agrees that both innovativeness and quality contribute to the firm's good financial performance and business success. The resource based view of the firm argues that a long-term competitive advantage of a firm depends on the inimitability, rarity, and non-tradability of its intangible resources (Penrose 1959). Cho and Pucik (2005) find that innovativeness not only has a direct relationship with quality, but also an indirect relationship with market value that is transmitted through quality.

Both Hendricks and Singhal (1996, 2001) find that product quality awards improve the firm's value creation over the long term. Our case confirms this branch of literature and reveals that Weixing signals their quality through pricing high and investing in research and development that continuously builds on their high-quality brand image in order to be able to charge a high price premium for their products.

Financial Situation

Weixing has achieved rapid growth since 2013. In 2017, the company created a revenue of RMB 3.903 billion (17.51% YoY increase), and a net profit of RMB 821 million (22.45% YoY increase). Figure 8.2 exhibits the company's EBITDA margin which increased every year from 2014 to 2017; the EBITDA kept increasing but at a decreasing rate in 2017.

Geographically, the sales revenue for east, north, west, northeast, and other areas accounted for 52%, 21%, 11%, 5% and 11%, respectively (Fig. 8.3). Figure 8.4 reveals the product sales increase in the past 4 years. In 2017, the company sold 198,000 tons of products, with a YoY increase of 11.3% in 2017; the company's selling expense per sales increased, while the main R&D costs increased 20.8%.

Weixing evolved itself into real production transformation and converted it into a high-tech manufacturer, built on high brand loyalty and a market leader position, which enabled Weixing to achieve a high profit growth in a highly competitive market even in the industry downturn.

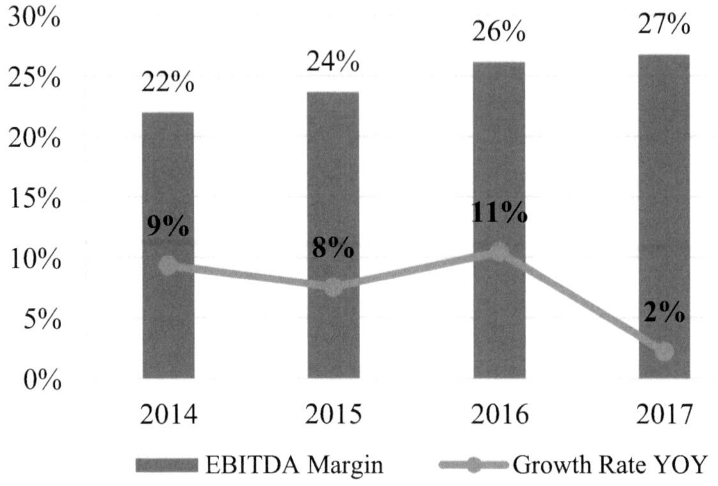

Fig. 8.2 EBITDA margin and growth rate

Fig. 8.3 Company regional revenue share in 2017

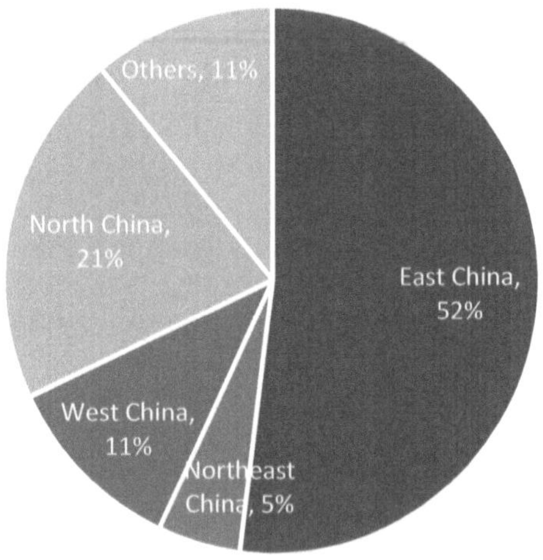

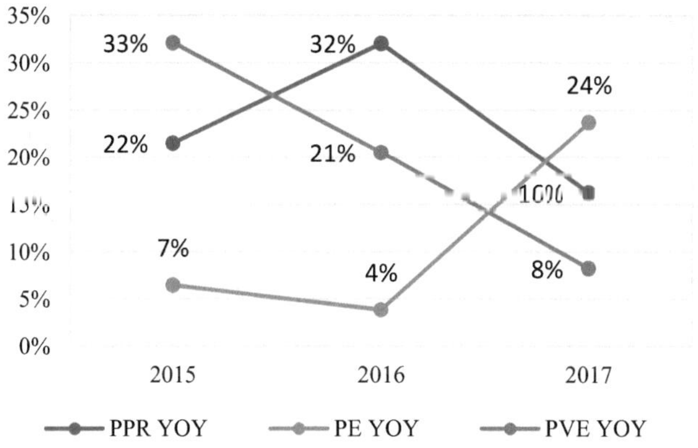

Fig. 8.4 Company product revenue and growth rate

Focusing on Core Business: Efficiency Management Through an Advanced Manufacturing Chain

Weixing places heavy emphasis on the quality of its products; "tri-inspection" is recognized through the entire manufacturing procedure without labor. This strengthens the inspection of the quality where defects can easily appear in the manufacturing process. While taking full advantage of the "full inspection" of the product, the company also increases the strength of "cross inspection", "sampling inspection", and "routine inspection". Since 2013, the company started its reform. In the process of production, it emphasizes the principle of high-quality products, and builds a production line combined with informationalization and industrialization, in order to carry out the unmanned automatic production model and complete the assembly and logistics system. These measures have achieved remarkable results in reducing cost and increasing efficiency. In 2017, the company profited greatly from its manufacturing upgrading; despite a 10% inflated raw material price and a 70% cost margin, its profit margin still reached 46.7% and achieved a significant profit growth of 22.45%. This success was mainly attributed to two reasons. First, the reduction of waste achieved through manufacturing automation. Second, the resulting bargaining power in the pipe market. As the leader of the industry, it has certain pricing power due to product differentiation and can also lay the foundation for the rapid growth of the company's profit. This confirms

Roy et al. (1994) who state that the leading enterprise in the industry plays an important role in pricing for the entire industry.

Building the Brand: The Wisdom "Product + Service" Initiation Penetrating Through the Company's Existing Retailing Channel

The barriers to entry in the plastic pipe industry are low. In the old "Steel Pipe" era, the quality of pipe was uneven and the production process significantly damaged the environment, which became a major problem in the industry. Over the past decade, plastic pipe gained in popularity around the world and gradually replaced the traditional steel pipe due to its lightweight and installation advantages. Weixing was one of the first adopters of the plastic pipe. In the "Plastic pipe" era, the customers benefitted from price competition from diverse product providers without understanding the quality of the product. As a result, the extensive industrial expansion led to overcapacity and low industry concentration, which made it difficult to establish a well-known brand. In addition, as the pipe is embedded inside the buildings, this makes promotion of the brand relatively difficult compared to more obvious consumption goods like home appliances, food, and beverages (Picture 8.2).

For the large manufacturers, setting up a recognizable brand is essential (De Chernatony 1989). The company created a marketing model so called "product + service" that enhanced the value of the product. As Weixing is known for its high-quality pipes, the attached free value-added service "star assistant" signals the brand value and solves the issue of the customer's ignorance of the quality of the pipes; it penetrates through the distribution channel and assists the end customers after the installation of the pipeline. This innovation not only changed the business model in the industry from "sell and ignore" to "sell and follow up", but also increased the entering barriers and set up a high standard to the industry. According to Purohit and Srivastava (2001), brand recognition of consumers has a significant impact on how consumers assess product quality. This highlighted the company's brand image of product quality. The initiation made the company's leading position more solid. The customers have become more loyal to Weixing's brands and associate the high price premium with high product quality.

Built on this brand value recognized through retailing, Weixing does not deliberately use advertising for promotion. Instead, they promote the

Picture 8.2 Weixing's poster

brand through the establishment of a deep marketing channel through promoting the brand review and recognition from the customers. In the areas surrounding Linhai, Tianjin, Chongqing, and other production bases, the company established more than 30 sales branches, with more than one thousand sales persons and over 20,000 marketing outlets all over the country, while the deepest penetration of the distribution network has reached the township level. Furthermore, it has established positive long-term collaborations with many design and decoration companies, well-known property development companies, water companies, and gas companies. Because of its low production cost, the company is able to sell at a smaller premium to retailer shops and large projects that enable higher gain to the downstream distributors. This strengthens their supply chain relationship, and the downstream dealers are more willing to promote Weixing's products to the terminal consumers. This new free add-on service strengthens the value even further.

Picture 8.3 "Star assistant" promotional poster

"Lead the marketing by brand, Support brand by service, and Enhance value though brand" is the core growth strategy of Weixing. The successful implementation of the strategy gives the company many rewards; the "Zhejiang Made" brand value assessment rewarded the company with a brand value of 912 out of 1000 points, ranking it 14th place in Zhejiang and 2nd place in the building materials and decoration industry with a brand value of RMB 5.44 billion (Picture 8.3).

Emphasizing R&D: Setup Industrial Benchmark Increased the Industry's Barrier to Entry

Weixing attaches great importance to R&D investment. It has established numerous laboratories and research centers including the national enterprise technology center, CNAS laboratory, China plastic pipeline engineering technology research and development center, Zhejiang post-doctoral workstation, and other important research and development platforms. This was accompanied by a strong R&D team specializing in technology development, product matching, system design, and application technology. The proportion of R&D outlay to the annual income is 3%. By the end of 2017, the company was awarded with over 460 patents and participated in the preparation of 82 national and industrial standards of which 46 industrial standards have been issued. In 2017 alone, the company's R&D

team's 23 research and development projects achieved another remarkable year, among which 9 projects were certified by the company and 4 projects were certified at the provincial level. In addition, 10 industrial standards were issued by the company, and 88 patents were in the application process among which 18 of the patents were invented patents. The company was awarded a number of prizes from the government including "Demonstrative enterprise for technological innovation in Zhejiang", "Excellent Zhejiang patent producer", and "Excellent Zhejiang industrial new product and new technology". This advanced technologic output established a large competitive advantage over its industrial peers.

Further Investigation

1. The pipe producing industry is a cyclical industry that moves with the economic cycle. The company suffered less compared to its peer firms and as a consequence the company gained from this industrial downturn. Explain why.
2. Describe how innovation and product quality can co-contribute to firm value creation.
3. The company expanded its distribution channel in light of a bonded supply chain relationship. How can a supply chain relationship benefit from a market leader's pricing power?
4. The company's R&D outlay in the short term produced less profit to the company, but it enhanced the product differentiation in the market. Explain the costs and benefits of this.

References

Akerlof, George A. "The market for 'lemons': Quality uncertainty and the market mechanism." In *Uncertainty in economics*, 235–251. New York, San Francisco, and London: Academic Press, 1978.

Cho, Hee-Jae, and Vladimir Pucik. "Relationship between innovativeness, quality, growth, profitability, and market value." *Strategic Management Journal* 26, no. 6 (2005): 555–575.

De Chernatony, Leslie. "Branding in an era of retailer dominance." *International Journal of Advertising* 8, no. 3 (1989): 245–260.

Dimoka, Angelika, Yili Hong, and Paul A. Pavlou. "On product uncertainty in online markets: Theory and evidence." *MIS Quarterly* 36 (2012): 395–496.

Hendricks, Kevin B., and Vinod R. Singhal. "Quality awards and the market value of the firm: An empirical investigation." *Management Science* 42, no. 3 (1996): 415–436.
Hendricks, Kevin B., and Vinod R. Singhal. "The long-run stock price performance of firms with effective TQM programs." *Management Science* 47, no. 3 (2001): 359–368.
Kirmani, Amna, and Akshay R. Rao. "No pain, no gain: A critical review of the literature on signaling unobservable product quality." *Journal of Marketing* 64, no. 2 (2000): 66–79.
Milgrom, Paul R., and Robert J. Weber. "A theory of auctions and competitive bidding." *Econometrica: Journal of the Econometric Society* 50 (1982): 1089–1122.
Pavlou, Paul A., Huigang Liang, and Yajiong Xue. "Understanding and mitigating uncertainty in online exchange relationships: A principal-agent perspective." *MIS Quarterly* 31 (2007): 105–136.
Penrose, Edith T. *The theory of the growth of the firm.* New York: Oxford University Press, 1959.
Porter, Michael E. "Industry structure and competitive strategy: Keys to profitability." *Financial Analysts Journal* 36, no. 4 (1980): 30–41.
Purohit, Devavrat, and Joydeep Srivastava. "Effect of manufacturer reputation, retailer reputation, and product warranty on consumer judgments of product quality: A cue diagnosticity framework." *Journal of Consumer Psychology* 10, no. 3 (2001): 123–134.
Roy, Abhik, Dominique M. Hanssens, and Jagmohan S. Raju. "Competitive pricing by a price leader." *Management Science* 40, no. 7 (1994): 809–823.

CHAPTER 9

Deli Group: A Five Force Behavioral Culture

Tiantian Zhang and Cherry Yi Zhang

Company Background

Deli Group, founded in 1988, was a small stationery manufacturer at the time. After 30 years of development, the company has evolved into a major market player in China's stationery industry. In the past decade, Deli converted their manufacturing site from a labor-intensive production to an unmanned factory, enabling the organization to achieve higher product quality and a more diversified assortment with a significant profit margin improvement. Their achievements are recognized with numerous high-quality brand awards, including the "National Inspection Exemption Certificate", "China's Top Ten Stationery Brands", "China best-selling stationery brand", "China well-known trademark", and other honorary titles (Picture 9.1).

The company is known for its behavioral orientated organizational culture, which highly aligns with their business operation. A term so-called "five force" led to a proud company. The five force makes the company

T. Zhang (✉) · C. Y. Zhang
University of Nottingham Ningbo China, Ningbo, China
e-mail: Tiantian.Zhang@nottingham.edu.cn

C. Y. Zhang
e-mail: Cherry-Yi.Zhang@nottingham.edu.cn

M. J. Liu and J. Luo (eds.), *China Branding*,
https://doi.org/10.1007/978-981-13-9318-1_9

Picture 9.1 Deli's promotional poster of its designer stationaries

strategically align their mission into five forceful dimensions consisting of product force, sale force, brand force, cultural force, and service force.

Organizational Culture and Brand Values

In Deshpande and Webster (1989), organizational culture is defined as "the pattern of shared values and beliefs that help individuals understand organizational functioning and thus provide them with norms for behavior in the organization". Many studies have shown that a good organizational culture will improve the firm's operational efficiency (Cameron 1985; Denison and Mishra 1995; Denison 1990; Gregory et al. 2009). The perceived organizational culture could be considered as organizational identity. It refers broadly to what members perceive, feel, and think about their organization. The organizational identity is considered as a collective, commonly shared understanding of the organization's distinctive values and characteristics. Empirical evidence suggests that members' beliefs about central and distinctive characteristics of their organization evolve in the face of internal stimuli. For example, Ravasi and Schultz (2006) reveal that organizational culture plays a vital role in supporting "sensemaking" action in an organization and shapes the members' shared understanding about the identity of the organization. Siehl and Martin (1989) suggested that culture affects employee attitudes which, in turn, has an impact on organizational effectiveness.

Organizational culture, identity, employee attitudes, organizational performance, and brand value are all interrelated. A well-developed organizational culture that shapes the employee's positive belief toward the organization's core value and identity, which could enable enhanced overall financial performance in the long run, can also lead to better brand recognition and reputation (Barth et al. 1998; Schein 1990).

Sirianni et al. (2013) demonstrate that overall customer brand evaluation increases when employees' behavior is aligned with the brand personality. Jo Hatch and Schultz (1997) argue that organizations should properly define their corporate identity and consider it as a bridge between the external position of the organization in its marketplace and other relevant environments, and internal meanings formed within the organizational culture. In fact, the strategic resource of the corporate brand (as measured by reputation) may partially reflect external perceptions of culture.

Product Force: Creative Product Design and Fundamental Innovation in Supply Chain Management

Starting with a local stationery factory in the coastal area of Zhejiang, Deli created a unique development path around its brand: through comprehensive development of an assortment of stationery, Deli benefited from high brand recognition and product awareness. Built on its solid foundation of brand awareness as well as earlier distribution channels, Deli has evolved from a manufacturer to a manufacturer brand. Deli's continuous optimization of its production and logistics function (Picture 9.2), as well as research and development input, strengthened its product force. As Page and Herr (2002) illustrate, the brand and design of a product have a significant impact on the quality judgment of the products. The value-added assortment development procedure so-called "Brand + Design + Product" development model helped Deli to gain numerous awards nationwide. The enabled product development model resulted in fruitful outputs. The company invested in research and development over 19 stationery categories, and that produced tens of thousands of value-added products. According to Leonard-Barton (1992), utilizing the key capabilities without being encumbered by their dysfunctional flip side, and innovation and change also play a significant role in the development of a new product.

Strategically, Deli aligns itself with well-known artists in their assortment development, which allows further market value improvement over a variety of products. Deli also invested over RMB145 million in supply chain facilities. In the process of production, the intelligent manufacturing reform has been adopted to improve production quality and efficiency and

Picture 9.2 Deli's unmanned factory

reduce production cost. In warehousing and logistics, Deli established a three-layer intelligent logistics system; with its headquartered warehouse in Zhejiang, Deli setup multidimensional distance-wise efficient logistics warehouses. All warehouses are well equipped with automated facilities and unmanned intelligent transportation management. The logistic facilities cover almost all parts of the country and enable 48-hour delivery. The consequence is a fully technologically optimized infrastructure and a stationery giant.

Sales Force: Strong Offline Distribution Channel Enabled Boosted Sales in the Digital Era

In the pre-digital era, Deli spent more than 30 years establishing its offline distribution channel (Picture 9.3). In the process of digital marketing transformation, the enterprise upgraded its distribution channel. First, it built sales networks to accurately match its production and distribution. With 76 wholesale branches throughout the country covering 34 provinces, 2877 cities, and counties, and connecting tens of thousands of retail outlets, the current distribution channel stimulates the growth of its online business. For the e-commerce channel, Deli has established cooperative relationships with Jing Dong, T-mall, Suning, and other e-commerce platforms, and through an advanced distribution model, it has achieved rapid development with current annual sales in two major platforms reaching around RMB2 billion each. For direct marketing channels, Deli established the "Deli mall" (business-to-business Direct sales service platform) and integrated tens of thousands of products. After years of development, the platform has established a cooperative relationship with many large well known enterprises, including PetroChina, Sinopec, the National Grid, and others. With regard to its overseas markets, Deli has set up regional exclusive distributors in the United States, Poland, United Arab Emirates, Russia, and India, in charge of the sales of their respective regions. So far, in some Southeast Asian countries, Deli has a dominant market share in the region. The spillover between online and offline distribution channels helped the enterprise maintain a high sales growth and provided the enterprise with the sharpest weapon in long-term development.

Brand Force: Cultivating Brand Recognition Among the Younger Generation Through Focused Market Segmentation

Due to the low entry barrier of the industry, brand is the easiest to have, while brand value is the hardest to build. Porter and Claycomb (1997) state that obtaining a favorable brand image is beneficial for the establishment of brand recognition. To improve its brand awareness, promotion strategies should be consistent with their brand image and product market segmentation. Deli's large-scale brand promotion began in 2009. So far, it has six core brands, each of which is at a different stage of its development. With a broad product assortment, Deli adopts different brand promotion strategies and uses a variety of promoting channels, including television, digital marketing, and offline sales to promote the products precisely to their target customers and maintain the brand awareness. "Deli Office" is the company's most reputable brand and contributes to the majority of the sales (Picture 9.4).

"Deli School" is a new designer brand targeted at Generation Z. For example, it obtained popular cartoon IP cooperation rights with Thomas, Xiaoming classmate etc., and its ads are shown in the Golden Eagle cartoon TV channels that are liked by kids and in a variety of internet video platforms' built-in drama advertisements that are favored by teenagers. This Generation Z promoting strategy leads the enterprise's growth without the risk of losing track of the young generation.

Picture 9.3 Deli's flagship store & exhibition center

Picture 9.4 "Deli Office" promotional poster

Service Force: Need Initiation, Research-Based Big Customer All Around Protection

It isn't always easy to add the right service factors to the product-leading industries, but once added, there will be a revolutionary change to the industry. According to Aurich et al. (2006), the technical service provided after sales allows effective feedback of the product performance. This is the innovative tech-service initiation that Deli is trying to promote and has named it "product + service new business model". In operation, Deli wants to improve the products with large data analysis from after-sales feedback to strengthen the efforts of customer service. Allowing the customer demand to lead the product will make the sale of their products achieve new records.

Cultural Force: Work, Live, Love Binding the Deli Culture

Discovered in the 1920s, the Human Relation Approach explains the informal relations among employers and employees and is concerned with moral and psychological rather than legal aspects of an organization. The approach considers workers as not only one of the means of the production system but as a man, which means focusing on the social well-being of the employees in an organization. According to Barney (1986), companies with good culture can achieve the expected financial performance while companies without a sound culture are likely to fail in achieving their goals.

Deli's long-term stable growth in its market size has greatly benefited from its human capital loyalty that is achieved by adopting a sound corporate culture: "To be a trustworthy and respected enterprise", and "Love Society, Love Enterprises, Love Products, Love Customers, Love Colleagues, Love Families"; the "Six Love" slogan has been embedded in everyone's belief in the enterprise. O'Reilly III et al. (1991) show that the satisfaction of employees will be reflected in the fit between employees and the organizational culture. The bounded relationship between the staff working in Deli has been strengthened through frequent team building opportunities organized within the organization; for instance, it prints their own "Deli Newspaper", holds seasonal sport competition events, as well as large-scale evening musical parties during festivals. All of these create excellent work and living environment for the staff. Employees approve of the enterprises, enterprises cherish employees, and this positive interaction produces a strong feeling of belonging and this well-developed people culture funded the rapid development of enterprises.

The Industrial Upgrading and Modernization Program

As a labor-intensive manufacturer, one of the most demanding challenges in the past decade is the significant rise in labor costs. In 2015, the stationery manufacturer's profit margin was only 3.18% on average in Zhejiang province, lower than the overall manufacturing sector by 2.5%. To cope with this difficulty, Deli optimized its operation through three upgrading dimensions. First, the production line upgrading. Deli strictly followed "Made in China 2025"'s strategic plan, completed the "replacing labor with machine" initiate and upgraded to unmanned factories (Picture 9.5). The adoption of a fully automated production line reduced a large portion of its production costs. Second, logistic upgrading. In order to overcome the problem of low efficiency in its logistic management, Deli adopted the exchange service of the national transport and logistics information platform and installed standardized management and logistic software. The outcome was rewarding. Deli enabled a Deli Group centered supply chain. The operational efficiency between Deli group and its external carriers

Picture 9.5 Deli's unmanned factory

increased by over 30%. This advanced logistics system greatly improved customer satisfaction. Third, upgrading sales through e-commerce. From 2010, Deli entered the online business market. They signed a strategic cooperation with Jing Dong in 2011 and gradually started their expansion in T-mall, Amazon, and other major e-commerce platforms. In the process of cooperation with the platforms, it gradually adopted the online marketing model, and actively participated in the e-commerce platform promotional activities. The O2O model that combines the advantage of the offline channel and online channel enabled the company to provide service offline to products sold online. Therefore, Deli strengthened its own leading position in the e-commerce channel. Deli experienced a rapid sales growth of 100% in the year 2012–2013. In the 2016 "single days"' sales, Deli won the sale's champion in the stationery sector in both the T-mall and Jing Dong platforms.

Further Investigation

1. Explain how organizational culture can be improved through a human relations approach in contrast to Taylor's Scientific Management approach.
2. Explain the difference between online and offline distribution channels.

3. What distribution mechanism can Deli extend to improve its performance?

References

Aurich, Jan C., Christian Fuchs, and Christian Wagenknecht. "Life cycle oriented design of technical Product-Service Systems." *Journal of Cleaner Production* 14, no. 17 (2006): 1480–1494.

Barney, Jay B. "Organizational culture: Can it be a source of sustained competitive advantage?" *Academy of Management Review* 11, no. 3 (1986): 656–665.

Barth, Mary E., Michael B. Clement, George Foster, and Ron Kasznik. "Brand values and capital market valuation." *Review of Accounting Studies* 3, no. 1–2 (1998): 41–68.

Cameron, Kim S. "Cultural Congruence, Strength, and Type: Relationships to Effectiveness. ASHE 1985 Annual Meeting Paper." 1985.

Denison, Daniel R. *Corporate culture and organizational effectiveness: Wiley series on organizational assessment and change*. Oxford: Wiley, 1990.

Denison, Daniel R., and Aneil K. Mishra. "Toward a theory of organizational culture and effectiveness." *Organization Science* 6, no. 2 (1995): 204–223.

Deshpande, Rohit, and Frederick E. Webster Jr. "Organizational culture and marketing: Defining the research agenda." *Journal of Marketing* 53, no. 1 (1989): 3–15.

Gregory, Brian T., Stanley G. Harris, Achilles A. Armenakis, and Christopher L. Shook. "Organizational culture and effectiveness: A study of values, attitudes, and organizational outcomes." *Journal of Business Research* 62, no. 7 (2009): 673–679.

Jo Hatch, Mary, and Majken Schultz. "Relations between organizational culture, identity and image." *European Journal of Marketing* 31, no. 5/6 (1997): 356–365.

Leonard-Barton, Dorothy. "Core capabilities and core rigidities: A paradox in managing new product development." *Strategic Management Journal* 13, no. S1 (1992): 111–125.

O'Reilly III, Charles A., Jennifer Chatman, and David F. Caldwell. "People and organizational culture: A profile comparison approach to assessing person-organization fit." *Academy of Management Journal* 34, no. 3 (1991): 487–516.

Page, Christine, and Paul M. Herr. "An investigation of the processes by which product design and brand strength interact to determine initial affect and quality judgments." *Journal of Consumer Psychology* 12, no. 2 (2002): 133–147.

Porter, Stephen S., and Cindy Claycomb. "The influence of brand recognition on retail store image." *Journal of Product & Brand Management* 6, no. 6 (1997): 373–387.

Ravasi, Davide, and Majken Schultz. "Responding to organizational identity threats: Exploring the role of organizational culture." *Academy of Management Journal* 49, no. 3 (2006): 433–458.
Schein, Edgar H. *Organizational culture*. Vol. 45, no. 2. American Psychological Association, 1990.
Siehl, Caren, and Joanne Martin. *Organizational culture: A key to financial performance?* Graduate School of Business, Stanford University, 1989.
Sirianni, Nancy J., Mary Jo Bitner, Stephen W. Brown, and Naomi Mandel. "Branded service encounters: Strategically aligning employee behavior with the brand positioning." *Journal of Marketing* 77, no. 6 (2013): 108–123.

CHAPTER 10

Unraveling the Myth of Futile: The Critical Role of Strategic Positioning in Brand Building

Liang (Lucas) Wang

Introduction

How to build a brand is of critical concern to all firms. A company's brand is one of its most important intangible assets. It signals the quality a product offers customers as well as bringing them psychological fulfillment when they use the product or services. Companies, therefore, rely heavily on the brand to attract and retain customers and boost sales. They can charge a premium price for the value a brand offers customers and this compensates brand-specific investments. Indeed, this premium price constitutes a substantial part of the total margin for some prestigious brands.

Brand building is particularly challenging for, but greatly desired by, Chinese manufacturing companies. In the past few decades, products made in China have pervaded the global market. Along the way, China first became the world's factory and then its second-largest economy. While this miraculous economic achievement is partly explained by institutional arrange-

L. Wang (✉)
University of Nottingham Ningbo China, Ningbo, China
e-mail: Lucas.Wang@nottingham.edu.cn

M. J. Liu and J. Luo (eds.), *China Branding*,
https://doi.org/10.1007/978-981-13-9318-1_10

ments, such as China's reform and open-door policy and its entrance into the WTO, the contributions of Chinese manufacturing companies—large and small—are undeniable. In particular, manufacturers located in Zhejiang Province made a wide array of products that have been exported to the furthest corners of the world; some even gained over 90% share of the global market. The dominance of Chinese products demonstrates strong production capabilities of Chinese manufacturers in quality control and cost reduction. With only a few exceptions, most of these products bear foreign brands—a situation arising from the overwhelming adoption of the Original Equipment Manufacturing (OEM) arrangement that governed the cooperation between Chinese manufacturers and developers from advanced economies. Without their own recognizable brands tagged on products, Chinese manufacturers have remained anonymous to customers, had constrained bargaining power vis-à-vis foreign collaborators, and ultimately claimed a tiny fraction of the total margins from sales. Thus, an urgent need arises for Chinese manufacturers to understand how they can build their own brands to gain both local and international awareness.

It is this need which motivates this study. Through an in-depth case analysis, the study aims to distil the useful approaches that Chinese manufacturers can learn and apply in their brand building processes. The case is Fotile Kitchenware Co. Ltd. (hereafter Fotile), which produces kitchen appliances (e.g., range hoods) and is among the few exceptional manufacturers that hold an independent high-end brand name in the industry. The strong brand reputation Fotile has enjoyed seems puzzling, even mysterious to many, given that most Chinese manufacturing companies in the kitchenware industry either do not have a brand or bear a non-recognizable one, and the high-end segment has been occupied by formidable foreign brands (e.g., Siemens). Hence, studying the process by which Fotile created and cultivated brand awareness will generate meaningful implications for Chinese manufacturers. A case study approach is adopted since this approach is widely regarded as the most suitable for the examination of process-based phenomenon (Yin 1984).

In the sections that follow, the literature on brand building is reviewed, then the methodology and the Fotile case are introduced. From inductive analysis of the case, a theoretical framework of the brand building process is developed which highlights strategic positioning as the initial condition and, perhaps, the most important factor of the whole process. The implications of this framework on the branding practices of companies and 'ZhejiangMade' policies are then discussed.

Literature Review

Brand names of goods or services became popular along with the rise of package trading in the early twentieth century (Shaw 1912). The use of packages, while necessary for preventing damage during handling and long-distance transportation, hampered buyers' capabilities to verify the quality of products before purchase. Quality, however, varied extensively from one manufacturer to another and buyers found it difficult to distinguish between products of good quality and those of poor quality. The anonymity of manufacturers conferred considerable power on middlemen in package trading to influence the purchasing decisions of customers and to claim the lion's share of the total profits. To remove the dictate of these middlemen and control more profits, manufacturers started to tag their products with a specific brand to appeal directly to customers. In fact, the rise of brand can be traced all the way back to ancient pottery trading where skilled potters stamped their output with a personalized trademark.

The pervasive use of brands did not escape the attention of scholars. Researchers of economics found that a brand serves as an effective mechanism to signal the quality of the goods or services to ill-informed customers (e.g., Zachary et al. 2011; Baumeister et al. 2015). It brings benefits to both sellers and buyers. Basing purchasing decisions on brand signals, customers reduce quality uncertainty in market transactions and save on searching costs. In addition, a brand offers a powerful means for customers to hold sellers accountable (Chiu et al. 2012; Chung et al. 2013; Monga and John 2010). They can reward a seller of reliable goods or services, or punish those sellers of poor quality by adjusting patronage or spreading the brand name via word of mouth. A recognizable brand, on the other hand, allows a seller to charge a premium price to compensate for investments committed to building the brand-specific reputation and awareness.

Studies from the marketing domain have looked at brand largely from the perspective of consumer psychology. In addition to quality signals in economics literature, marketing scholars uncovered that certain brands can bring customers psychological fulfillment which affects their purchasing behaviors. Customers can derive such fulfillment directly from using the goods or services tagged with a brand (e.g., underwear from Victoria's Secret) (Möller and Herm 2013), or by projecting to others the desired image that the brand stands for (e.g., a luxury brand to showcase wealth) (Chernev et al. 2011; Choi and Winterich 2013). For such psychological satisfaction, customers are willing to pay a premium to reward the seller who successfully endows the desirable identity and resonance with a brand. This element of 'premium price' is often categorized as 'brand equity' (Dolbec and Chebat 2013; Whan Park et al. 2010).

If brand is so valuable to the sale of products, how firms build a brand becomes an important concern. To this inquiry, marketing scholars have identified various processes and practices of brand building. Broadly speaking, these practices fall into two sequential and interconnected steps. The first is to create brand salience. Customers will only start associating meaning to a brand if they can easily recognize it among all other brands (Lam et al. 2010). In other words, a brand must stand out in the perception of customers. This is often achieved by repeated exposure to the brand image (e.g., TV commercials and advertising boards). Next, firms must create and associate a clear identity with the brand which is unique and endorsed by target customers. If successful, customers then establish a strong bond with the brand and remain loyal to the firm (Whan Park et al. 2010; Zachary et al. 2011).

Research from both economists and marketing scholars is undoubtedly insightful regarding the function of a brand and the process of brand building. These two research streams, nonetheless, bear certain limitations. Economic theorists have been preoccupied with explaining how the use of brand reduces quality uncertainty and facilitates market transactions. Their analysis started with the brand as a given condition, thereby omitting the preceding process of creating and building an appealing brand. Although marketing research has extensively examined brand building, most analysis has centered on the individual level interactions between brand images and psychological perceptions and purchasing behaviors of customers. As a result, these two research streams shed limited light on brand building in terms of firm-level strategies. In other words, the economics research is too macro and the marketing research is too micro to have direct and practical implications on the formulation and implementation of a firm's strategies toward brand building.

Also documented in literature is that the lack of knowledge on brand building strategies at the firm level is particularly salient to Chinese manufacturing companies. Recent decades have seen the rise of these companies to become a formidable powerhouse in global production and international trade. These companies have been famed for their low-cost production and low prices of goods or services. To access the low-cost factors in China, many foreign companies decided to outsource their production component to Chinese manufacturers through OEM contracts. It is common to observe that Chinese manufacturing companies receive orders along with a specified design from abroad, produce the goods locally, and ship them to foreign locations. Leveraging cost advantages and the progression of international trade, some Chinese manufacturing companies have taken a large share of the global market in their respective output—some even over 90%. Beneath this impressive achievement is the hidden truth that Chinese manufacturing companies only claim a tiny fraction of the total profits from their products. One major and often-cited reason is the absence of a brand for Chinese manufacturers to tag on their output. Without a recognizable brand, Chinese manufacturers remain anonymous to the final buyers. This not only significantly weakens their bargaining power vis-à-vis foreign outsourcing collaborators, but also bars them from charging a brand-specific premium.

Therefore, to Chinese manufacturers and various levels of government, the pressing question is: what are the strategies for a Chinese manufacturing company to build a brand? An adequate answer cannot be found among economics and marketing research due to the aforementioned limitations. Thus, this study attempts to bridge this knowledge gap by analyzing the case of Fotile.

Method: Case Study

A case study methodology is adopted in this research. According to Eisenhardt and Graebner (2007), 'case studies are rich, empirical descriptions of particular instances of a phenomenon that are typically based on a variety of data sources (p. 25)'. A case study serves as a distinct real-life experiment and case analysis identifies the key constructs, the patterns of relationships among these constructs, as well as the mechanisms responsible for them. Unlike experiments in laboratories that separate a phenomenon from its context, case analysis of a company can bring rich context into theorization, allowing the exploration of the interactions between firms' practices and contextual influences. Not surprisingly then, case study has been widely considered as the most suitable qualitative approach to examine the process-based phenomena in the business arena (Yin 1984).

For a single-case analysis, it is important to collect information from multiple sources. Information from more than one source allows a researcher to capture multiple relevant aspects of a focused phenomenon, as well as verifying information and eliminating biases through triangulation. This study, therefore, drew extensive information about Fotile from a wide range of sources, including the company's website, news reports, books, scripts, and secondary databases.

Company Background of Fotile

Fotile was founded in Cixi, Zhejiang Province, China, in 1996. The two co-founders were Zhongqun Mao, then a freshly minted graduate student, and his father who founded and was running Feixiang Group, the largest producer and exporter of ignition torches in the world. Fotile began by manufacturing and marketing range hoods to Chinese households. By the time Fotile entered the industry, most other incumbent Chinese producers had been replicating the existing models of foreign hoods in order to avoid the costs and risks of R&D. In contrast, Fotile chose to design its own models from the very beginning and targeted its products at the high-end segment of the market. Fotile's founder Mao explained this counterintuitive strategic choice.

> The high-end segment of Chinese home appliances was dominated by few foreign brands whereas the low-end segment was crowded with numerous local Chinese brands. Yet, despite their high price, foreign range hoods could not satisfy the demands of Chinese customers due to the extra greasy fumes of the Chinese way of cooking. An ambitious dream thus arose: we will make Fotile the first high-end brand of range hoods in China and prove to the world that Chinese can also produce high-quality range hoods.[1]

This high-end positioning of Fotile, coupled with independent R&D, was later proved successful by its explosive growth. Only three years after its foundation, Fotile had turned into a major brand in the Chinese kitchen appliance industry. It held the second largest market share and quickly became a household name—a reputation that Fotile has maintained to date. Shortly afterwards, Fotile has grown into a leader in kitchen appliances in China with the largest annual revenue in the industry. In 2017, it was the first company in the kitchenware industry to surpass the milestone of ¥15 billion annual sales. It dominated the high-end kitchen appliances segment with over 40% market share.

Along with its successful and impressive performance, the Fotile brand also earned wide publicity and recognition. In 2011, it won the 'Chinese Brand of the Year' from CCTV, China's national TV station. Between 2009 and 2016 it has continuously remained the most honored brand in the kitchen appliances industry, according to the 'Chinese Company Brand

[1] http://m.eeo.com.cn/2019/0316/350600.shtml, accessed on March 18, 2019.

Survey' administered by CBNweekly. In 2017, Fotile was the only brand from the kitchen appliances industry that was admitted into the National Brand Plan, a program supported by the Chinese central government to recognize and support outstanding Chinese brands.

Product Development

Starting with range hoods, which are still a strong business line for Fotile, the company has diversified into other kitchenware, including stoves, ovens, dishwashers, steamers, microwaves, and tableware disinfectors.

Range Hoods

Fotile launched its first range hood, A Model, in 1996. This model featured a deep hood with a curly and smooth inner shell. The deep hood significantly increased the suction effect by expanding the areas under the hood. The filtrated oil which usually dropped down directly onto the stove could now slip to the edge of the shell and be cleaned with little effort. Another unique feature of the A Model was that the inner shell could be easily detached from the hood, and customers could wash it with water without worrying about electric shocks. These innovative features pushed the price of A Model to $120, higher than the most expensive hood in the market at the time, which was $100. Despite the high price and the anonymity of the Fotile brand, more than 30,000 units of A Model were sold in the first year. This instant success motivated Fotile to update A Model into Q Model in 1997.

The success of A Model would not have been possible if not for the perseverance and commitment of the R&D team led by Mao. The development of A Model took eight months, whereas the development of a product was typically no more than three months. The extra time taken was to realize Mao's vision to make Fotile's hoods function better and look prettier. Accordingly, the R&D team included not only engineers who worked on technological sophistication, but also two industrial designers who emphasized the appearance of the hood. The R&D director reflected on the R&D project of A Model,

> Fotile was the pioneer in China that emphasized industrial design in product development. Chinese families put more demands on the elaborate design of home appliances as they get wealthier. Only recently has the government

started to push for the innovation on both technology and industrial design. We realized these two forces 20 years ago.[2]

European Model

After Q Model, Fotile put forth its first European-style range hoods in 2001. The European Model featured a reversed 'T' shape and used stainless steel as its main material. Since it reflected the elegant taste and even the wealth of buyers, this hood could also serve as a key decoration in the kitchen. Nonetheless, the European model provided an insufficient suction effect in Chinese kitchens, so Fotile's R&D modified the internal structure of the European Model and installed a more powerful motor to increase its suction effect. That way, Fotile's European-style hood was the only one on the market that successfully combined the elegant look of the European Model with sufficient suction power.

Another important innovation of Fotile's European hood was a cone-shaped filtration net. Before Fotile, most filtration nets on foreign-branded European models on the market had a flat net with no device to store filtrated oil, so the filtered oil dripped directly down to the stove. To solve this problem, Fotile's team invented the cone-shaped net. Using this net, the oil could be channeled to the bottom of the net where a small container was installed to hold the oil. This feature turned out to be especially useful in Chinese kitchens and the cone-shaped net became an industry standard to date. Fotile's European Models were priced at around $400, while the average hood was no more than $120. Despite this higher price, Fotile sold over 10,000 units of European hoods in the first year of launch.

Wind Magic

If the deep range hoods, A and Q Models, and the European hoods were made through incremental modifications to existing products, the side-suction range hood was an authentic innovation by Fotile introduced in 2009. This product line was dubbed 'Wind Magic'. Unlike all previous range hoods that hung above the stove, Wind Magic was attached to the side-wall close to the stove and sucked fumes from the side rather than from the top of the stove. The initial motivation was to reduce the space taken

[2] http://www.lexiangjiadian.com/dianqi/6677, accessed on February 20, 2019.

up by a range hood in order to fit the small kitchens of Chinese apartments; but the side suction turned out to work even more effectively than all other types, thanks to the shorter distance from the source of the fumes. Wind Magic sold over 40,000 units in the first year of its launch. In fact, with Wind Magic, Fotile opened up a new market segment in the range hood history

Diversification into Other Kitchenware

After establishing its range hood business, Fotile began to diversify into other related product lines. In 2004, it launched its first water heater which used gas for fuel. While heaters in foreign countries were large and took up a whole basement room, Fotile's heater was small and could be fitted into the small Chinese kitchens.

In 2005, Fotile added two more kitchenware categories, specifically stoves and tableware disinfectors. The stove was uniquely designed to be embedded into the counter and the disinfector into the cabinets. This embedded design saved space, offering a crucial benefit in small Chinese kitchens. It also enhanced the consistency and integration of kitchen appliances with other components in the kitchen, thereby fulfilling increasing demands among the Chinese for elaborate and elegant decoration of their kitchens. Fotile made the stove and the disinfector in stainless steel as with their European range hoods. These three categories of kitchenware, with their consistently silver-like look, formed a set dubbed 'Galaxy 3'. This marked the beginning for Fotile to market its products as a set.

In 2008, Fotile's product family was further expanded to incorporate microwaves and ovens. These two appliances were also made of stainless steel and could be embedded. They formed 'Silverwise 5' alongside Fotile's range hood, stove, and disinfector. In 2009, Fotile added a steamer and started a set called 'Lightshadow 6'.

In 2015, Fotile launched its sink dishwasher. All dishwashers on the market, local or international brands, were European style and were too large for the small kitchens in China. To fit them under the counter, the height of the counter needed to be raised, which created a problem for Chinese housewives who, on average, tend to be shorter than Western women. Also, Chinese kitchens normally have only one sewer outlet which is often designated for the sink. It would require the installation of additional pipes to link the dishwasher to the sewer. European-style dishwashers were also unfriendly for seniors as they require them to bend down to put tableware

FOTILE 方太

Fig. 10.1 Fotile's brand

into the washer. The solution from Fotile to all these problems is the sink dishwasher. This washer is integrated with the sink and, therefore, takes no additional space in the kitchen, it is at the same height as the countertop, and it uses the same sink pipe to discharge water. In addition to washing dishes, it can be used to wash off pesticide residues from vegetables and fruits.

Brand Evolution of Fotile

Fotile's Chinese brand name is 'Fang Tai'. Fang was drawn from the Chinese word 'Fangbian' which means convenience. Tai is a word for housewives in Chinese. Hence, the brand 'Fang Tai' was naturally linked with the kitchen and resonated with 'bringing convenience to housewives' (Fig. 10.1).

In 1997, Fotile made a TV commercial to promote its new brand. This turned out to be one of the best commercials in China. The commercial was starred by a famous TV anchor of a popular cooking show in Hong Kong. The anchor was also widely recognized as 'Fang Tai'—exactly the same as Fotile's Chinese brand name. This was the first business commercial where the brand ambassador and the product brand shared the same name. The commercial line, 'cooking with Fang Tai and eliminating fumes with Fotile' became an instant hit, making Fotile a household name in the kitchen appliance industry. In the year the commercial was released, the sales of Fotile's range hoods increased by over 200% from the previous year, reaching $30 million.

Using a celebrity in commercials offered a shortcut for Fotile to enhance its brand reputation. However, it also raised Fotile's dependence on an individual person, which can be risky for a business firm. To remove the celebrity effect on its brand reputation, Fotile rolled out a new branding campaign in a press conference in 2003. The marked change in the campaign was that Fotile upgraded its image from 'Fotile Kitchenware' to 'Fotile Kitchen Expert'. This extended brand image accurately reflected the strategic shift of Fotile from a manufacturer of a single kitchenware item (i.e., range hoods) to a leading and more diversified producer of elite kitchen appliances.

Fotile's brand saw another significant evolution in 2009. In this year, embedded design became the distinctive theme of Fotile's product development as all its kitchen appliances, except range hoods, were designed to be embedded into countertops, walls, or cabinets. To be consistent with the embedded design theme, Fotile then changed its brand image from 'Kitchen Expert' to 'Embedded Kitchen Electric Appliance Expert'. This new image portrayed a more focused and distinctive positioning of Fotile in the market.

A Dynamic Process of Brand Building: Strategic Positioning, Product Development, and Brand Building

Fotile is now the most valued brand in the kitchen appliance industry with a large group of loyal customers in China and across the world. The success of Fotile in building its brand is particularly impressive in the light of two observations in the industry. For one, most Chinese manufacturers, some of which entered the industry much earlier or were more resourceful than Fotile, have failed to cultivate a brand with comparable recognition. These manufacturers are now mainly working as a subcontractors for their OEM clients abroad with little share of final profits. For the second observation, the Chinese kitchen appliance industry was not without strong foreign competitors. Leveraging their established brand reputation and deep pockets, foreign competitors, such as Siemens from Germany, have made many attempts to dominate the kitchen appliance market, but eventually all were defeated by Fotile. Indeed, Fotile is one of the few manufacturers in China that have thrived in the competition with foreign rivals. To both Chinese and foreign competitors, the rise of Fotile as the top brand has become a myth. The question is how to unravel it.

By looking into the developmental path of Fotile, a pattern with three inter-linked and sequential components emerges. This at least partly explains the success of Fotile in developing its brand from unknown to market leader (Fig. 10.2).

The three components of this pattern behind Fotile's success are strategic positioning, product development, and brand building. Among the three, *strategic positioning* is the starting point and, perhaps, the most important component at every critical turn Fotile has made (Paharia et al. 2014). At the very conception of this company, the leadership and man-

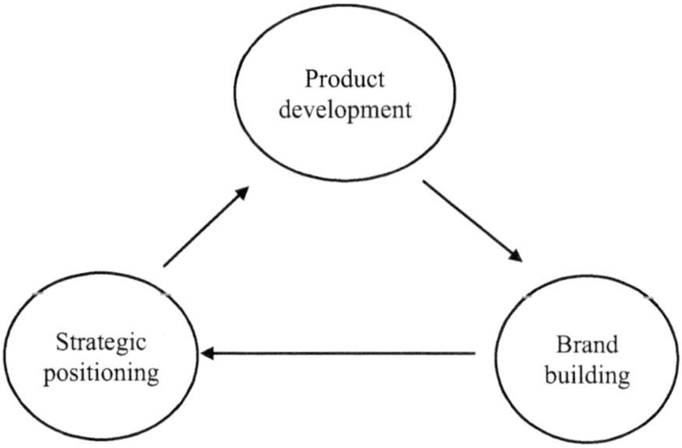

Fig. 10.2 Positioning-development-branding model

agement were keen to observe a niche in the range hood market where no competitor existed, i.e., the high-end market segment. Although this segment had been occupied by foreign brands, these brands fell short of their suction effect in Chinese kitchens. Hence, customer demands were unfulfilled. This positioning then gave rise to the goal that guided the *product development*, i.e., to enhance the suction effect of range hoods to satisfy the unique demands of Chinese customers. The solution was the first deep hood in the industry from Fotile. Brand building through the successful TV commercial, which accurately highlighted the powerful range hoods from Fotile, followed. With the rise of brand recognition, the strategic positioning was secured.

This positioning-development-branding framework not only explained the successful experience of A and Q Models (Phase 1 in Fig. 10.3), but can also be applied to explain the other two branding initiatives undertaken by Fotile (Phases 2 and 3).

As Fotile increasingly focused on the high-end market, the brand 'Fotile Kitchenware' no longer fitted its strategic positioning. So, Fotile diversified into new product lines—stoves and disinfectors—and offered the three products together as a combo to the market (i.e., Galaxy 3). To reflect this strategic shift, Fotile then rebranded itself as the 'Kitchen Appliances Expert'.

The strategic positioning was further specified when Fotile focused not only on the high-end segment, but also on embedded design. In other words, Fotile further departmentalized the high-end segment by concentrating on a specific niche. Guided by this positioning, product development then emphasized an embedded design, and the branding campaign

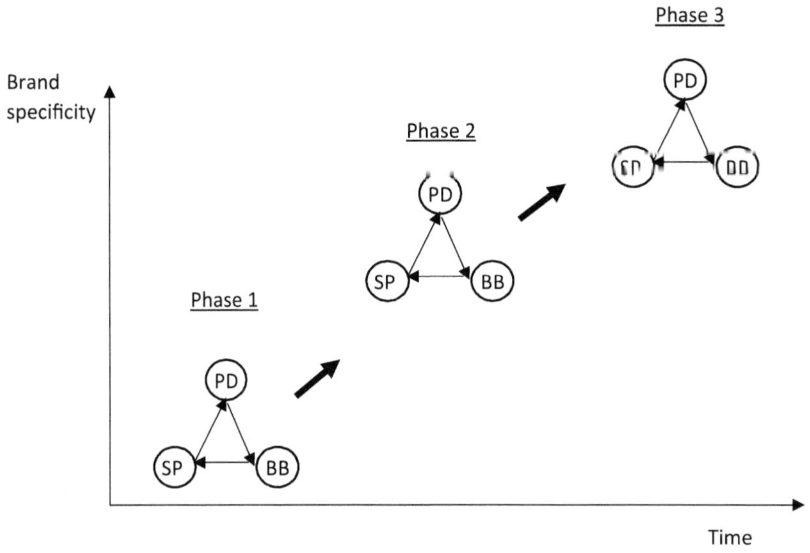

Fig. 10.3 Three phases in Fotile's branding

then followed to reimage Fotile as the 'Embedded Kitchen Appliances Expert'.

Implications of the Fotile Case

Following the analysis in the previous section, the success of Fotile in the kitchen appliances industry becomes less mysterious. At least partly, the branding strategies of Fotile can be categorized into three interconnected components, strategic positioning, product development, and brand building. This framework exerts meaningful implications on the branding practices of Chinese manufacturers and the Zhejiang Government in promoting the brand of 'ZhejiangMade'.

Implications for Manufacturing Companies

Brand building should be taken as a strategic initiative. While brand management is usually allocated to the marketing department in a company, it takes strategic positioning as the starting point to drive the whole process. Hence, identifying a fitted strategic positioning in the product market is crucial to the cultivation of a brand. After all, if the positioning is wrong, competition can be too fierce to withstand, especially for Chinese manufacturers who started as anonymous subcontractors. In this case, brand building would not save the business, let alone the brand, and abundant resources would be wasted.

Companies should not look at brand building as a stand-alone practice. Instead, a holistic view should be taken to consider strategic positioning, product development, and brand building. More important, perhaps, is to pay attention to the consistency and coherence among these three components. If a company fixes on a market position, the development of suitable products to satisfy the demands of that position should follow and so should branding strategies. Notably, as in Fotile's case, a company can shift its position along the way and this means companies need to retain a certain level of strategic flexibility and also be able to rebrand themselves accordingly.

Implications on 'ZhejiangMade'

To some extent, the above implications of manufacturing companies also apply to government officials when they attempt to promote the brand 'ZhejiangMade'. While strategic thinking and a holistic perspective are two important elements, two additional implications for government policy can be drawn here.

Firstly, 'ZhejiangMade' is still a brand, even though it is not related to a specific product or owned by a single company. It is suggested that government officials explore the strategic position behind this brand. How do the products bearing the 'ZhejiangMade' brand fit into the global market? Do they have clearly targeted customers with specialized needs? How can these products or services satisfy these needs? Only when answers to such questions are found, and the positioning of Zhejiang manufacturing clarified, will the 'ZhejiangMade' brand be successfully built and maintained.

Secondly, the 'ZhejiangMade' brand is not simply a label; its reputation rests on consistently solid quality goods and services provided by manufacturers in Zhejiang, such as Fotile. From an institutional level, government agencies should formulate policies to guide manufacturers to locate the right strategic position of their output, strengthen product or service development and then, accordingly, create and nurture their brands. At the bottom line, 'ZhejiangMade' will only be as strong and reputable as the brands of the manufacturing companies in Zhejiang.

Further Investigation

1. What are the factors that led Mao to determine the high-end positioning for Fotile?
2. What is the evolution path of Fotile's brand?
3. What are the pros and cons of extending Fotile's brand from a range hood business to include other kitchen appliances (e.g., stove, steamer, disinfector, and microwave)?
4. What are the potential threats to the positioning of Fotile and the effective strategic responses?

References

Baumeister, Christoph, Anne Scherer, and Florian V. Wangenheim. "Branding access offers: The importance of product brands, ownership status, and spillover effects to parent brands." *Journal of the Academy of Marketing Science* 43, no. 5 (2015): 574–588.

Chernev, Alexander, Ryan Hamilton, and David Gal. "Competing for consumer identity: Limits to self-expression and the perils of lifestyle branding." *Journal of Marketing* 75, no. 3 (2011): 66–82.

Chiu, Hung-Chang, Yi-Ching Hsieh, and Yi-Chu Kuo. "How to align your brand stories with your products." *Journal of Retailing* 88, no. 2 (2012): 262–275.

Choi, Woo Jin, and Karen Page Winterich. "Can brands move in from the outside? How moral identity enhances out-group brand attitudes." *Journal of Marketing* 77, no. 2 (2013): 96–111.

Chung, Kevin Y. C., Timothy P. Derdenger, and Kannan Srinivasan. "Economic value of celebrity endorsements: Tiger Woods' impact on sales of Nike golf balls." *Marketing Science* 32, no. 2 (2013): 271–293.

Dolbec, Pierre-Yann, and Jean-Charles Chebat. "The impact of a flagship vs. a brand store on brand attitude, brand attachment and brand equity." *Journal of Retailing* 89, no. 4 (2013): 460–466.

Eisenhardt, Kathleen M., and Melissa E. Graebner. "Theory building from cases: Opportunities and challenges." *Academy of Management Journal* 50, no. 1 (2007): 25–32.

Lam, Son K., Michael Ahearne, Ye Hu, and Niels Schillewaert. "Resistance to brand switching when a radically new brand is introduced: A social identity theory perspective." *Journal of Marketing* 74, no. 6 (2010): 128–146.

Möller, Jana, and Steffen Herm. "Shaping retail brand personality perceptions by bodily experiences." *Journal of Retailing* 89, no. 4 (2013): 438–446.
Monga, Alokparna Basu, and Deborah Roedder John. "What makes brands elastic? The influence of brand concept and styles of thinking on brand extension evaluation." *Journal of Marketing* 74, no. 3 (2010): 80–92.
Paharia, Neeru, Jill Avery, and Anat Keinan. "Positioning brands against large competitors to increase sales." *Journal of Marketing Research* 51, no. 6 (2014): 647–656.
Shaw, Arch Wilkinson. "Some problems in market distribution." *The Quarterly Journal of Economics* 26, no. 4 (1912): 703–765.
Whan Park, C., Deborah J. MacInnis, Joseph Priester, Andreas B. Eisingerich, and Dawn Iacobucci. "Brand attachment and brand attitude strength: Conceptual and empirical differentiation of two critical brand equity drivers." *Journal of Marketing* 74, no. 6 (2010): 1–17.
Yin, Robert K. *Case study research: Design and methods.* Beverly Hills, CA: Sage Publications, 1984.
Zachary, Miles A., Aaron F. McKenny, Jeremy C. Short, Kelly M. Davis, and Di Wu. "Franchise branding: An organizational identity perspective." *Journal of the Academy of Marketing Science* 39, no. 4 (2011): 629–645.